**MEDICAL SERIES**
**COURTROOM DRAMAS**
**SPY DRAMAS**
**ADVENTURE SERIES**
**POLICE DRAMAS**
**WESTERN SERIES**
**DETECTIVE DRAMAS**
**SCIENCE FICTION SERIES**
**WAR DRAMAS**
**GENERAL DRAMAS**
**SITCOMS OF THE '50s**
**SITCOMS OF THE '60s**
**SITCOMS OF THE '70s**
**NEWSPAPERS**
**ANIMAL SERIES**

and much, much more

# TV Trivia

Fred Miranda
& Bill Ginch

BALLANTINE BOOKS • NEW YORK

To my beautiful wife, Debbie, whose help and support were instrumental in making this book a reality. The joys of life aren't really appreciated until you have someone special to share them with. I am truly blessed to have found Debbie. To the BAMFS, the greatest group of guys you could ever meet. Playing ball with them makes each game enjoyable and each loss inevitable. Long live the BAMFS! To Edward L. Norton, Ralph Kramden's buddy and pal, for inspiring this whole crazy thing!

—F. M.

To my wonderful mother, Margaret, who is always there when I need her, in good times and in bad. To my late father, Sgt. Charles Ginch of the N.Y.P.D. Without their help and guidance throughout the years this book would not have been possible. To my good friends back in Mayfield, who inspired this crazy idea many years ago—Wally, Eddie, and of course the Beaver.

—B. G.

Library of Congress Catalog Card Number: 84-90622

ISBN 0-345-32005-0

Manufactured in the United States of America

First Edition: November 1984

# TABLE OF CONTENTS

INTRODUCTION ... 1

DOCTOR! DOCTOR! ... 3
   Trivia questions based on TV medical dramas

ORDER IN THE COURT! ... 14
   Trivia questions based on TV courtroom & law
   dramas

HOW INTRIGUING! ... 23
   Trivia questions based on TV spy & espionage
   dramas

HOLD ON TO YOUR HATS! ... 34
   Trivia questions based on TV adventure series

STOP IN THE NAME OF THE LAW! ... 45
   Trivia questions based on TV police dramas

PUT THE WAGONS IN A CIRCLE! ... 56
   Trivia questions based on TV Western series

STAKE-OUT! ... 67
   Trivia questions based on TV detective dramas

OUT OF THIS WORLD! 76
Trivia questions based on TV science fiction series

WHICH WAY TO THE FRONT? 84
Trivia questions based on TV war dramas

GENERALLY SPEAKING . . . 89
Trivia questions based on TV general dramas

STOP THE PRESSES! 98
Trivia questions based on TV newspaper dramas

MAKE 'EM LAUGH! 103
Trivia questions based on TV sitcoms of the 1950s

KEEP 'EM LAUGHING! 118
Trivia questions based on TV sitcoms of the 1960s

THEY'RE STILL LAUGHING! 136
Trivia questions based on TV sitcoms of the 1970s

TELEVISION'S BEST FRIEND 153
Trivia questions based on TV animal series

TELEVISION'S GRAB BAG! 157
Trivia questions based on a little of everything

TOTAL TV OBSCURITY 162
Trivia questions only an expert can answer

ANSWERS 173

INDEX 251

# INTRODUCTION

We feel absolutely obsessed with the need to tell you, right off the bat, why we wrote this book. It all began one day not very much different from any other. We were talking about how television programming has been going rapidly downhill over the past few years and how great it would be if we could recapture the magic that television represented throughout the 1950s, 1960s, and, to some extent, the 1970s and 1980s.

As we tossed series titles at each other we both realized that the fond memories we had of these television series of years ago were seemingly endless. Each new title we mentioned brought us back a little further to a time when we rushed home to spend a part of our lives with our favorite television families. Agreeing that there was no way we could remember all the programs that we enjoyed so much, we decided to compile this book so that others may take that magical trip back to a time when television was the king of entertainment.

What better way, we thought, to get people thinking than to ask them some questions based on these great television programs of the past? We by no means attempt at this time to tell you we have covered every millimeter of film from every show. Instead, what we feel we have done is light a fire that can grow with your memory as its only fuel.

On the following pages you will find trivia questions on a

great many of the television programs that aired in these four magical decades. Of course, you won't remember every show, but we are sure that you will be very surprised, as we were, at just how many of these programs you do remember. Doing this book has been a true labor of love and a real learning experience for us both. We have unlocked our minds, and the memories that were inside were found to be quite priceless, but they are no more valuable than the ones you will undoubtedly uncover on your magical journey.

The departure point for this journey will differ from reader to reader, but we believe that you will bump into one another at least a few times along the way. Maybe you'll all meet in Mayfield, where you might drop in on the Cleavers. Maybe your meeting point will be Bryant Park, where you might stop for a visit with Steve Douglas and his three sons.

For those of you who crave some excitement, perhaps you will run into some fellow travelers aboard the U.S.S. *Enterprise* as you help Captain Kirk pilot his craft through one or another far-off galaxy. Perhaps you'll bump into one another aboard the *Seaview*, that beautiful submarine with Admiral Nelson at the helm. Maybe a few of you will get "Lost in Space" with the Robinsons.

Whichever of these explorations you do undertake, however, we want to assure you that you will be well protected on your journey. With the likes of Batman, Superman, and the Green Hornet around, you have to know that you're safe. And just for an added measure of precaution, we'll throw in two personal bodyguards, Toody and Muldoon, from the New York City Police Department!

As you can see by now, there's nothing for you to do except to let your memories flow. We hope you gain even a small fraction of the enjoyment that we did in writing this book. Our chief concern is that people will forget all about these great old shows; that would be a tragedy indeed. We want to keep these programs in your mind always as a remembrance of how great television once was.

Whether or not you answer these questions correctly is absolutely the least important aspect of this book. Just toss a sheet over the television in your living room and turn on the one in your mind. Travel with us on our magical journey and remember. And enjoy!

# DOCTOR!
# DOCTOR!

**H**OW CAN ONE SIMPLY EXPLAIN THE FASCINA-tion that television viewers have had with the medical drama over the years? There are a few schools of thought on this subject and we probably agree with all of them to some extent. Which of these theories do you think is most accurate in pinpointing the popularity of the medical drama?

1. *People don't really mind human suffering as long as it isn't their own.* Most people probably don't have any qualms about sitting through an hour of someone else's pain and anguish. TV illness is not that hard to take, because, after all, it is only a television program. However, in recent seasons, the medical drama has taken on a much stronger sense of reality, and now perhaps the harder it is to watch a medical drama, the finer a job the program is doing in conveying that reality.

2. *People need to feel compassion, and the TV medical drama gives them an outlet in which to do*

*so*. It's probably not easy for most people to show compassion to others in today's society, where every spare minute can easily be filled with countless more important things to do. However, the C.Q. (Compassion Quota) can be met one hour a week by tuning in to your favorite medical drama. A seemingly endless array of poor souls will fill your living room. Simply pick one and open up that great big heart of yours! Just think: if you get all of your compassion out of the way early in the week, you can go back to being your miserable self.

3. *The characters are totally irresistible.* Since the beginning of medical drama time, the characters have been made so righteous, handsome, and moral that it is hard for anyone not to fall madly in love with them, let alone watch their programs. Once again, it is only recently that a look into a doctor's private life might uncover something terrible. For years, TV doctors were the epitome of purity, and that was very hard to resist indeed. Not only did they save all these lives from week to week, but they found time to pet a dog, buy an ice cream cone for a little kid, or go to church twice a day!

All of these theories probably give some indication why the medical drama always has been very popular on television. Based on this popularity, we have assembled some questions on medical dramas that have come into your living rooms on more than one occasion. Hold your hand steady now! Find a competent staff to assist you as you operate on the following.

BEN CASEY   (1961–1966, ABC)

1. Who played Dr. Ben Casey?

2. For the 1965–1966 season, a major cast change occurred. Dr. David Zorba, Casey's mentor, left the series and was replaced by Dr. Daniel Niles Freeland. Who played both these roles?

3. Who discovered the star of this series? (His production company produced the series.)

4. On the series, Casey had a love affair of short duration with Jane Hancock. Who played her, and from what sickness had she recovered?

5. Love was also hinted on occasion between Casey and Dr. Maggie Graham. She was played by what actress?

Answers on page 175.

## BREAKING POINT   (1963–1964, ABC)

1. Who played chief resident psychiatrist, Dr. McKinley Thompson, on this series?

2. By what nickname was Dr. Thompson known to his staff?

3. His superior, Dr. Edward Raymer, the director of the hospital's psychiatric clinic, was played by what actor?

Answers on page 175.

## CITY HOSPITAL   (1952–1953, CBS)

1. Who played medical director Dr. Barton Crane?

2. Seeing a female doctor was strange for this early stage of television, but "City Hospital" had one. She was Dr. Kate Morrow. What actress played her?

3. What two shows were included, along with "City Hospital," in a three-program package shown on an alternating basis?

Answers on page 175.

## DOC ELLIOTT   (1974, ABC)

1. What veteran actor played the title role in this series?

2. In the series, Dr. Benjamin Elliott gave up his career in New York City to practice in what city?

3. By what means of transportation did Doc Elliott make his house calls?

4. Who played Mags Brimble, the doctor's confidante and friend?

5. Why was the producer of this series unique?

Answers on pages 175–176.

## THE DOCTOR   (1952–1953, NBC)

This series had only one leading role; the rest of the major roles were played by guest stars each week. Who played "The Doctor"?

Answer on page 176.

## DOCTORS' HOSPITAL   (1975–1976, NBC)

1. Dr. Jake Goodwin was played by what veteran actor?

2. What was Dr. Goodwin's official title?

3. The chief resident, Dr. Felipe Ortega, was played by what actor?

Answers on page 176.

## DOCTORS' PRIVATE LIVES   (1979, ABC)

1. What type of doctors were the two lead characters, Dr. Michael Wise and Dr. Jeffrey Latimer?

2. Who played Dr. Michael Wise and Dr. Jeffrey Latimer?

Answers on page 176.

## DR. HUDSON'S SECRET JOURNAL (1955–1957; syndicated)

Dr. Wayne Hudson was played by what actor?

Answer on page 176.

## DR. KILDARE (1961–1966, NBC)

1. "Dr. Kildare" ran concurrently with "Ben Casey" on ABC. These medical series were two of the finest made and most popular ever presented on television. Who played the handsome Dr. Kildare?

2. Casey had a mentor, and so did Kildare. Dr. Leonard Gillespie was played by what distinguished actor?

3. What programming change did the series undertake for the 1965–66 season?

4. Dr. Kildare's two hospital buddies (1961–1962 only) were Dr. Simon Agurski and Dr. Thomas Gerson. Who played these two doctors?

5. The series was known for its realism and later in its television life it took on the look of today's television phenomenon, the mini-series. For how many episodes did the longest of these multi-episode story lines run?

Answers on page 176.

## DR. SIMON LOCKE (1971–1974; syndicated)

1. Who played Dr. Simon Locke?

2. As in every medical drama worth its weight in stethoscopes, Dr. Locke had a mentor. Who played Dr. Locke's superior, Dr. Sellers?

3. To what was the series title changed in its final season?

Answers on page 176.

## THE ELEVENTH HOUR (1962–1964, NBC)

1. In this series dealing with psychiatry, two doctors shared one office. They were Dr. Theodore Bassett (1962–1963) and Dr. Paul Graham. Who played these roles?

2. Which actor took over for Dr. Bassett in the second season in the role of Dr. L. Richard Starke?

Answers on page 176.

## HAVING BABIES (1978–1979, ABC)

1. What actress played the lead role in this series?

2. By the fourth episode, the series title had been changed. What was the new title?

3. Who played the older, experienced Dr. Blake Simmons?

Answers on page 177.

## THE INTERNS (1970–1971, CBS)

1. Who starred in this series in the role of Dr. Peter Goldstone?

2. Dr. Goldstone was the father figure to five young interns, one of whom went on to fame in one of television's all-time greatest situation comedies. He played Dr. Sam Marsh. Who was he?

Answers on page 177.

## JANET DEAN, REGISTERED NURSE   (1953–1954; syndicated)

Who played the title role in this short-lived series?

Answer on page 177.

## THE LAZARUS SYNDROME   (1979, ABC)

1.  Who played the lead role of Dr. MacArthur St. Clair?
2.  What was Dr. St. Clair's official title?
3.  Who played his wife, Gloria?
4.  What is the Lazarus Syndrome?

Answers on page 177.

## MATT LINCOLN   (1970–1971, ABC)

1.  What former star of a medical series returned to star in this series?
2.  What type of service did Matt Lincoln run?
3.  What was the name of the service?
4.  Who played Tag, Matt's female helper?

Answers on page 177.

## MEDIC   (1954–1956, NBC)

Who played the role of Dr. Konrad Styner, the lead character and narrator of this series, whose story lines were based on actual case histories?

Answer on page 177.

## MEDICAL CENTER   (1969–1976, CBS)

1.  Who played the role of Dr. Joe Gannon?

2. Once again we find that our doctor hero has an older associate to guide him through each episode. In this case, he was Dr. Paul Lochner. What actor played him?

3. Aside from being an associate professor of surgery, Dr. Gannon took on some added responsibilities in the second season. What were they?

4. Who played the very efficient Nurse Wilcox?

5. Nurse Chambers was played by what veteran actress?

Answers on page 177.

## THE NEW DOCTORS   (1969–1973, NBC)

1. "The New Doctors" began as part of what multi-program package?

2. Who played the leading role on the series?

3. Dr. Paul Hunter was played by an actor who later played a schoolteacher. Who was he?

4. The chief of surgery, Dr. Ted Stuart (1969–1972), was played by what actor?

5. What was Dr. Stuart's specialty?

Answers on pages 177–178.

## NOAH'S ARK   (1956–1958, NBC)

1. Why was this medical series different from all the others?

2. A veteran of many television series played the role of Dr. Noah McCann. Who was he?

3. His partner, Dr. Sam Rinehart, was played by what actor?

4. What famous television actor directed this series?

Answers on page 178.

## NURSE   (1981, CBS)

1. Who played the lead role of Nurse Mary Benjamin on this short-lived series?
2. Her friend, Dr. Kenneth Rose, was played by a veteran series actor who had once played the role of a father of six. Who was he?

Answers on page 178.

## THE NURSES   (1962–1965, CBS)

1. This series centered around the lives of two nurses at a metropolitan hospital. Who played nurses Liz Thorpe and Gail Lucas?
2. When two doctors became prominent characters in the series, the title was changed in 1964. What was the new title?

Answers on page 178.

## THE PSYCHIATRIST   (1971, NBC)

1. "The Psychiatrist" was part of which four-series package?
2. Who played Dr. James Whitman, the psychiatrist?

Answers on page 178.

## RAFFERTY   (1977, CBS)

1. Sid Rafferty, M.D., the lead character in this series, was played by what actor?
2. Rafferty served for many years as a doctor in a branch of the United States military. Which branch?

Answers on page 178.

## WESTSIDE MEDICAL   (1977, ABC)

The series centered around three doctors who opened their own clinic in Southern California in order to provide personalized and specialty care for their patients. What actors played Dr. Sam Lanagan, Dr. Janet Cottrell, and Dr. Philip Parker?

Answers on page 178.

Please take the following MEDICAL EXAMINATION!

Just match the TV Medical Series with the Hospital used for its setting.

1. "Ben Casey" (1961–66, ABC)
2. "Dr. Kildare" (1961–66, NBC)
3. "Marcus Welby, M.D." (1966–76, ABC)
4. "The New Doctors" (1966–73, NBC)
5. "The Interns" (1970–71, CBS)
6. "Doctors' Hospital" (1975–76, NBC)
7. "The Lazarus Syndrome" (1979, ABC)
8. "The Nurses" (1962–67, CBS)
9. "Having Babies" (1978–79, ABC)
10. "Nurse" (1981, CBS)
11. "Rafferty" (1977, CBS)
12. "Breaking Point" (1963–64, ABC)

a. Hope Memorial Hospital
b. Alden General Hospital
c. New North Hospital
d. York Hospital
e. Blair General Hospital
f. Grant Memorial Hospital
g. Webster Memorial Hospital
h. City General Hospital
i. County General Hospital
j. Lowell Memorial Hospital
k. Lake General Hospital
l. David Craig Institute of New Medicine

Answers on page 178.

## MASTER QUIZ

## MARCUS WELBY, M.D.   (1969–1976, ABC)

One of the most popular medical series in television history, "Marcus Welby, M.D.," reached its audience through the kind and compassionate Dr. Welby and the handsome good looks of his assistant, Dr. Steven Kiley. The show dealt with important topics and informed viewers as well as entertained them. Here is a master quiz on this very popular series.

1. What actor played the kindly Dr. Welby?

2. What previous series did he star in years earlier?

3. Steven Kiley, Dr. Welby's assistant, was played by what actor?

4. Loyal secretary Consuelo was an important member of this strong cast. What was her last name, and who played her?

5. In what city was Dr. Welby's practice?

6. Dr. Welby's home was used as the home of another famous family in a series some years before. What family lived there?

7. For only a brief time during the first season, a love interest for Dr. Kiley was worked into the show. What was her name, and what actress played the role?

8. Later in the series, Dr. Kiley got married to the hospital's public relations director, Janet Blake. What actress played the role of Janet Blake?

9. Dr. Welby's daughter was played by Ann Schedeen. What was her name on the show?

10. What child actor played Dr. Welby's six-year-old grandson?

Answers on pages 178–179.

# ORDER IN THE COURT!

HERE'S NOTHING LIKE A GOOD COURTROOM drama to keep you on the edge of your seat, and that's exactly how viewers responded to the courtroom drama over the years. It is very possible to imagine millions of viewers leaning forward, staring into the television, and wondering how one or another case might turn out. It's true that the guilty were usually punished and the innocent exonerated, but nevertheless, those millions of viewers tuned in week after week to sweat out yet another case with their favorite TV attorneys.

This section is devoted to both the courtroom drama, which dealt mainly with the actual trials themselves, and the law drama, which gave you an insight into the life of a particular lawyer from the time of the commission of the crime through the trial, with everything in between.

We are now ready to begin our interrogation of the witness (that's you), so be reminded to tell the truth, the whole truth, and nothing but the truth! And please don't be alarmed if when you reach the very end of the chapter and there seems to be no hope, Paul Drake rushes in to hand you that vital piece of information to help you triumph as he did for Perry Mason week after week after week.

## ACCUSED (1958–1959, ABC)

1. "Accused" was a spinoff of what show?
2. Who played the presiding judge, and why was he unique?

Answers on page 179.

## THE BLACK ROBE (1949–1950, NBC)

1. Who played the judge and the police officer on this series?
2. The story lines were taken from case histories from what type of court in what city?

Answers on page 179.

## THE D.A. (1971–1972, NBC)

1. Who played Paul Ryan, and what was his official title?
2. Chief Deputy D.A. Stafford was played by what actor? What was his nickname on the series?
3. What was the Public Defender's name on the series, and what actress played the role?
4. What character did Ned Romero play?

Answers on page 179.

## THE DEFENDERS (1961–1965, CBS)

1. What was the relationship between Lawrence Preston and Kenneth Preston on "The Defenders"?
2. What law firm did they work for?
3. Who played the role of Joan Miller, Kenneth's girl friend?

4. "The Defenders" was based on one episode of "Studio One." Who played the two lead roles in that episode?

Answers on page 179.

## HAWKINS (1973–1974, CBS)

1. What actor played the role of lawyer Billy Jim Hawkins?

2. His assistant, R. J. Hawkins, was played by what veteran actor? What was his relationship to Billy Jim Hawkins?

Answers on pages 179–180.

## JUDD FOR THE DEFENSE (1967–1969, ABC)

1. What was Judd's first name?

2. What actor played the title role in this series?

3. Judd's assistant, Ben Caldwell, was played by what young actor?

Answers on page 180.

## JUSTICE (1954–1956, NBC)

1. On what agency's files were the story lines for "Justice" based?

2. Who produced this series?

Answers on page 180.

## KATE McSHANE (1975, CBS)

1. Who starred in the lead role as Kate McShane? (She was a veteran comedienne trying a dramatic role.)

2. Why was this series unique?

3. Who played Kate's father, Pat McShane, on the series?

Answers on page 180.

## THE LAW AND MR. JONES  (1960–1962, ABC)

1. What was Mr. Jones's full name, and who played him?

2. Who played the part of law clerk C. E. Carruthers?

Answers on page 180.

## THE LAWYERS  (1969–1972, NBC)

Who played the three lawyers in this series, which was part of *The Bold Ones*?

Answer on page 180.

## LOCK-UP  (1959–1961; syndicated)

1. Who played lawyer Herbert L. Maris in this syndicated series?

2. Who played Maris's secretary, and how was she known on the series?

3. What was the real-life relationship of these two actors?

Answers on page 180.

## OWEN MARSHALL, COUNSELOR AT LAW  (1971–1974, ABC)

1. Who played the title role in this very popular series?

2. What actor, who later starred in his own series, played Jess Brendon, his law partner?

3. Who played other law partners Danny Paterno (1973–1974) and Ted Warrick?

4. Frieda Krouse was Owen's loyal law clerk throughout the show's run. Who played that role?

5. Who played Marshall's wife, and who played his daughter on the show?

6. In a rare happening, Marshall defended what character from what other ABC show in a lawsuit?

Answers on pages 180–181.

## PETROCELLI   (1974–1976, NBC)

1. Who played the lead role of lawyer Tony Petrocelli?

2. What college had Petrocelli graduated from?

3. What actress played Maggie Petrocelli, Tony's wife in the series?

4. What type of home did the Petrocellis have?

Answers on page 181.

## THE PUBLIC DEFENDER   (1954–1955, CBS)

1. Who was the public defender?

2. What unique occurrence took place on every episode of this series?

Answers on page 181.

## ROSETTI AND RYAN   (1977, NBC)

1. Who played the title roles in this series?

2. Who played Assistant District Attorney Jessica Hornesby?

3. What was Frank Ryan's occupation before he became a lawyer?

Answers on page 181.

## SAM BENEDICT   (1962–1963, NBC)

What veteran actor played the title role of Sam Benedict?

Answer on page 181.

## STOREFRONT LAWYERS   (1970–1971, CBS)

1. Who played the roles of the three lawyers who went into partnership on this series?

2. What firm did David Hansen leave to join forces with his two colleagues?

3. Five months after the show's debut, the title was changed to what?

4. What law firm did the three work for in the show's second season?

Answers on page 181.

## THEY STAND ACCUSED   (1949, CBS; 1950–1954, Dumont)

1. By what title was this series originally known?

2. What was unique about the scripts for this series?

3. What was unique about the cast of this series?

4. Immediately before each show, someone had to brief the participants on the plot. Whose job was that on "They Stand Accused"?

Answers on page 181.

## TRAFFIC COURT   (1958–1959, ABC)

The cast was simply known as "The Judge," "Bailiff," and "Court Clerk." Do you know who acted these roles?

Answer on page 182.

## TRIALS OF O'BRIEN   (1965–1966, CBS)

1. Who played the lead role of Daniel J. O'Brien?

2. O'Brien's beautiful ex-wife, Katie, was played by what actress?

3. By what name was O'Brien's secretary known on the show?

4. What actor played Lieutenant Garrison?

Answers on page 182.

## THE VERDICT IS YOURS   (1958, CBS)

In this series, real court cases were reenacted by real lawyers and judges, with members of the audience passing the verdicts. A court reporter was provided to keep viewers abreast of the situations. Who was he?

Answer on page 182.

## WILLY   (1954–1958, CBS)

Who played lawyer Willa Dodger in this series?

Answer on page 182.

## THE WITNESS   (1960–1961, CBS)

1. What type of criminal did this show go after in particular?

2. Who was the court reporter in this series?

Answers on page 182.

You're under oath, so take this quiz without any cheating. Just match the show with the city in which it was set.

| | |
|---|---|
| 1. "Judd for the Defense" (1967–69, ABC) | a. Los Angeles |
| 2. "Petrocelli" (1974–76, NBC) | b. New York |
| 3. "Sam Benedict" (1962–63, NBC) | c. Renfew, New Hampshire |
| 4. "Storefront Lawyers" (1970–71, CBS) | d. Houston |
| 5. "Trials of O'Brien" (1965–66, CBS) | e. San Francisco |
| 6. "Willy" (1954–55, CBS) | f. San Remo |

Answers on page 182.

## MASTER QUIZ

## PERRY MASON   (1957–1966, CBS)

"Perry Mason" was the longest-running lawyer series in television history. Week after week, viewers would tune in to watch Perry pull victory from the jaws of death and win yet another case, most times at the last possible moment.Take this quiz or serve the maximum sentence.

1. Who played the title role of Perry Mason?

2. Who played Perry's loyal secretary, and what was her name on the show?

3. Perry's very able assistant, Paul Drake, was played by what actor?

4. Who created this very popular series?

5. Did Perry Mason ever lose a case?

6. After seven years on the air, a remake of this classic series appeared on television. What was its title?

7. In the remake, who played the title role of Perry Mason?

8. His secretary still went by the same name, but what actress played her from 1973 to 1974?

9. Paul Drake, as effective an assistant as ever, was played by what actor?

10. Name the two actors who played District Attorney Hamilton Burger in the original series and in the remake.

Answers on pages 182–183.

# How Intriguing!

WE FEEL IT SAFE TO SAY THAT TELEVISION VIEWers have always been intrigued by intrigue. The spy or espionage drama satisfies a need we all have, the need for excitement. Unfortunately most of us can't take time off from our humdrum jobs and jet off to Europe to hobnob with the elite and romance the beautiful people while all the time attempting to solve another brilliant crime. Most of us cannot afford to live dangerously, so we must have someone else do it for us. The spy drama takes all these desires and packs them into an hour of chills and thrills for us to enjoy vicariously, through one hero or another.

The most notable element of the spy drama is the overall and ever-constant sense of romance—romance not only in the sense of "I'm a man and you're a woman," although that type of romance certainly plays a major role, but in the sense of romance of life itself. There doesn't seem to be one single boring minute in the day for our TV heroes!

So if you're like us, read on and relive some of those exciting TV moments that supplemented our lives every week as we tried so desperately to forget about how routine our lives were in reality. We feel safe in the assumption that you will find the following questions very intriguing.

## ASSIGNMENT VIENNA   (1972–1973, ABC)

1. This series was one of three in a multi-program package. What was it called?

2. Back once again in a starring role, he played international spy Jake Webster. Who is he?

3. What was the name of the business Jake Webster ran in Vienna?

4. Where was this series filmed?

5. Major Caldwell of U.S. Intelligence was played by what actor?

Answers on page 183.

## THE AVENGERS   (1966–1969, ABC)

1. Throughout its original three-year run and then again when the series was remade in 1976, one man remained constant to the cast. He played Jonathan Steed. Who was he?

2. What was the 1976 remake of "The Avengers" called?

3. Who was Steed's original partner in the British version of "The Avengers"?

4. Steed had two partners from 1966 to 1969. The first was played by Diana Rigg. What was her series name?

5. The second partner was Tara King. Who played the role?

6. Why did Rigg's character leave the show?

7. Who played "Mother," Steed's superior?

Answers on page 183.

## THE BARON   (1966, ABC)

1. Who played John Mannering, aka "The Baron"?
2. What types of shops did he own, and where were they located?

Answers on page 183.

## BEHIND CLOSED DOORS   (1958–1959, NBC)

Who played the lead role of Commander Matson?

Answer on page 183.

## BLUE LIGHT   (1966, ABC)

1. Who starred as David March in this spy drama?
2. Can you name the countries in which this series was filmed?
3. What was the actual name of the secret organization March belonged to?

Answers on page 183.

## CASABLANCA   (1955–1956, ABC)

1. Rick Jason, made famous by Humphrey Bogart in the movies, was played by what actor in this series?
2. What was the name of the club Rick owned?

Answers on page 184.

## CRUSADER   (1955–1956, CBS)

1. Freelance writer Matt Anders was played by what actor?
2. For what cause did Matt Anders fight?

Answers on page 184.

## DANGER MAN   (1961, CBS)

1. What actor played Danger Man John Drake?
2. With what real-life agency was Danger Man associated?

Answers on page 184.

## DANGEROUS ASSIGNMENT   (1951–1952; syndicated)

Who played the lead role of Steve Mitchell in "Dangerous Assignment"?

Answer on page 184.

## THE DELPHI BUREAU   (1972–1973, ABC)

1. Who played the lead role of Glenn Garth Gregory in this series?
2. His government connection was Sybil Van Loween. What actress played this role?

Answers on page 184.

## DOORWAY TO DANGER   (1951–1953, NBC and ABC)

1. By what title was the series known in its first season?
2. A different actor played the role of John Randolph in each of the three years this series was on the air. Can you name them?

Answers on page 184.

## ESPIONAGE   (1963–1964, NBC)

This anthology series featured different actors each week. On what continent was this series filmed?

Answer on page 184.

## FIVE FINGERS   (1959–1960, ABC)

1. Who played American counterspy Victor Sebastian?
2. What was Victor Sebastian's code name?

Answers on page 184.

## FOREIGN INTRIGUE   (1951–1955; syndicated)

1. What did this series's production have in common with so many other spy dramas?
2. From 1951 to 1953 the lead role was that of Robert Cannon. What actor played him?
3. The lead role from 1953 to 1954 was that of Michael Powers. What actor played him?
4. What actor played Christopher Storm?

Answers on page 184.

## THE GIRL FROM U.N.C.L.E.   (1966–1967, NBC)

1. From what show was "The Girl from U.N.C.L.E." a spinoff?
2. Who played the lead role of April Dancer?
3. Alexander Waverly was the organization head of U.N.C.L.E. What actor played this role?

Answers on page 185.

## HUNTER  (1977, CBS)

1. Who played the title role of James Hunter in the series?

2. His partner, Marty Shaw, was played by what actress? (She later reached great heights in another series.)

3. Hunter's supervisor, General Baker, was played by an actor who played a president in the movies. Who was he?

Answers on page 185.

## THE HUNTER  (1952–1954, CBS and NBC)

The lead character, Bart Adams, was played by what two actors in this series's run?

Answer on page 185.

## I LED THREE LIVES  (1953–1956; syndicated)

1. What three lives did Herbert Philbrick lead?

2. What actor played the role of Herbert Philbrick?

3. In what metropolitan city was Herbert Philbrick based?

4. Who played Eva Philbrick, Herbert's wife?

5. There were two regulars in the cast who played special agents. One was Special Agent Dressler and the other Special Agent Henderson. What two actors played these roles?

Answers on page 185.

## I SPY  (1965–1968, NBC)

1. The two lead roles in "I Spy" were played by what two actors?

2. Why was this show significant?

3. What cover did these agents use in traveling world-wide solving crimes?

Answers on page 185.

## THE INVISIBLE MAN   (1958–1960, CBS)

1. Who played Peter Brady, the invisible man?
2. How were Diane Brady and Sally Brady related to Peter in the show?

Answers on page 185.

## IT TAKES A THIEF   (1968–1970, ABC)

1. What actor starred in the role of government spy Alexander Mundy?
2. What was his profession before becoming a spy?
3. Where did Mundy serve his jail sentence?
4. Who played Alexander's father, Alister Mundy?

Answers on pages 185–186.

## A MAN CALLED SLOANE   (1979–1980, NBC)

1. Back in another short-stay television series, this veteran actor starred as the title character. Who was he?
2. What was Sloane's full name?
3. Who played his trusted aid, Torque?
4. Featured on the show was an E.F.I. Multifunction computer affectionately called "Effie." Who was the voice of "Effie"?

Answers on page 186.

## THE MAN CALLED X   (1955–1956; syndicated)

What actor played the role of Agent Ken Thurston?

Answer on page 186.

## THE MAN FROM U.N.C.L.E.   (1964–1968, NBC)

1. The two super-agents featured here were suave Napoleon Solo and sexy Illya Kuryakin. What actors played these roles?

2. From what country was Illya Kuryakin?

3. Toward the end of this series the secretary of Alexander Waverly (he was played by Leo G. Carroll) became much more prominent in the cast. Who played Lisa Rogers (1967–1968)?

Answers on page 186.

## THE MAN WHO NEVER WAS   (1966–1967, ABC)

1. Who played American espionage agent Peter Murphy in this series?

2. Who was Mark Wainwright?

3. Who played the role of Eva Wainwright, the series wife?

Answers on page 186.

## PASSPORT TO DANGER   (1954–1956; syndicated)

Who played the role of agent Steve McQuinn in this series?

Answer on page 186.

## RENDEZVOUS (1952, ABC)

1. What foreign-born actress played the lead role of night-club owner–spy Nikki Angell in this series?
2. What was the name of her nightclub?

Answers on page 186.

## THE RHINEMANN EXCHANGE (1977, NBC)

1. This series was one-quarter of a set of novels made into a series by NBC. What was their collective title?
2. Lead character David Spaulding was played by what actor?
3. The female interest was Leslie Hawkewood. Who played her?
4. Who played Erich Rhinemann? How about General Swanson? Bobby Ballard? Maybe Walter Kendall? Or perhaps Ambassador Granville?

Answers on page 186.

## THE SAINT (1967–1969, NBC)

1. What handsome actor played the lead role Simon Templar from 1967 to 1969?
2. In the 1978 remake, who played Templar?

Answers on page 187.

## SECRET AGENT (1965–1966, CBS)

John Drake, Danger Man in the series of the same name, returns here in "Secret Agent." What actor plays him this time around?

Answer on page 187.

SHADOW OF THE CLOAK   (1951–1952, Dumont)

Who played the lead role of chief agent Peter House?

Answer on page 187.

THE THIRD MAN   (1959–1962; syndicated)

What actor played the role of Harry Lime, crime-solver?

Answer on page 187.

The Good Guys And The Bad Guys

Some people don't know "good" from "bad." If you were forced to join one of these agencies, which would you choose? Simply pick which of these represent the "good guys" and which are the "baddies."

1. I.M. FORCE
2. K.A.R.T.E.L.
3. T.H.R.U.S.H.
4. N.A.T.O.
5. U.N.C.L.E.
6. U.N.I.T.

Answers on page 187.

**MASTER QUIZ**

MISSION IMPOSSIBLE   (1966–1973, CBS)

From every angle, starting with the nifty theme and down to the closing credits, this was a totally popular series. It was done with a flair for professionalism and attention to detail that is sadly missing from most of today's television programs.

Changing time slots seven times and changing nights four times, it maintained its loyal audience throughout its run and it is still seen in syndication nationally.

Here is a master quiz on probably the most popular intrigue series in television history.

1. The lead role was that of James Phelps from 1967 to 1973. What actor played him?

2. For the initial season, Jim Phelps was not in the cast. The lead character was Daniel Briggs. He was played by what actor?

3. What husband-and-wife team appeared on the show regularly? What were the characters' names?

4. Who played Barney Collier? Willie Armitage?

5. In the "broads with brains" category, three women shared the role from 1970 to 1973. Can you name them?

6. What actor played Paris (1969–1971)?

7. How long did it take the tape to self-destruct at each show's opening?

8. What was Barney Collier's specialty?

9. What special skill did Rollin Hand possess?

10. Who wrote the theme song for "Mission Impossible"?

Answers on page 187.

# HOLD ON TO YOUR HATS!

NE THING THAT WE ALL SEEK AT FAIRLY REGular intervals is adventure. Outwardly or subconsciously, it is a desire we all have had at one time or another. Adventure is such an all-encompassing word; it cannot really be defined without a great deal of debate, so we will not attempt to do so. Instead, we will try to study how television brought adventure into our lives each week.

As we said, it is nearly impossible for us to define "adventure," and television couldn't define it either, so I guess we're in good company. All the series on which you will be quizzed on the following pages are recognized as adventure series, but as you will find, no two are quite the same. Within this chapter, which is dedicated solely to adventure series, you will find everyone from Tarzan to Batman, from Mr. Lucky to the Bionic Woman. There were no criteria for the adventure series on television. As long as it was exciting, people would watch, and that pretty much was the case.

As you can see, there is no pattern here, that is what makes the adventure series so much fun. No pattern, no rules, just one spontaneous burst of excitement and one action after another. So just grab on to the nearest swinging vine and head for the truly adventurous questions that lie just ahead.

## THE AMERICAN GIRLS   (1978, CBS)

1. Who played the lead roles of Rebecca Tomkins and Amy Waddell?
2. What fictitious TV program did they work for?
3. The girls traveled around the country, but in what city were they based?

Answers on page 188.

## BIG HAWAII   (1977, NBC)

1. What was the name of the ranch used as a setting on this show and who owned it?
2. Who played Mitch, the only son of the ranch owner?

Answers on page 188.

## THE BIONIC WOMAN   (1976–1978, ABC and NBC)

1. What was the Bionic Woman's name, and who played her?
2. What was her profession before becoming Bionic Woman?
3. What was the Bionic Woman's hometown?
4. What government offices did the Bionic Woman work for?

Answers on page 188.

## BORN FREE   (1974, CBS)

1. Where was this series filmed?

2. Who played George and Jan Adamson?

3. What was the name of the lioness prominently featured on the show?

Answers on page 188.

## DAKTARI  (1966–1969, CBS)

1. Who played Dr. Marsh Tracy in the series?

2. Where was this series filmed?

3. What does "Daktari" mean?

4. Who played orphan girl Jenny Jones (1968–1969)?

Answers on page 188.

## THE GREEN HORNET  (1966–1967, ABC)

1. What was the Green Hornet's real name? Who played him?

2. What was the name of the Green Hornet's car? What make was it?

3. What newspaper did the Green Hornet own in everyday life?

4. Who played the role of the Green Hornet's sidekick, Kato?

Answers on page 188.

## THE IMMORTAL  (1970–1971, ABC)

1. Who was the immortal, and who played the role?

2. What made him immortal?

3. Who played millionaire Arthur Maitland?

Answers on page 189.

## LUCAN   (1977–1978, ABC)

1. Who played the title role in this series?
2. Where did the name "Lucan" come from?

Answers on page 189.

## THE MAGICIAN   (1973–1974, NBC)

1. Who was the magician, and who played him?
2. Who played his friend Max Pomeroy, and what was his profession?
3. What was the name of the magician's airliner?

Answers on page 189.

## THE MAN FROM ATLANTIS   (1977–1978, NBC)

1. Who was Mark Harris, and who played him?
2. Harris agreed to help with project experiments at what research center?
3. Who played Dr. Elizabeth Merrill, the one who found Harris?

Answers on page 189.

## MR. LUCKY   (1959–1960, CBS)

1. Who played Mr. Lucky, and what was his profession?
2. What was the name of his floating casino?
3. Who played Mr. Lucky's best friend, Andamo?
4. Who wrote the series's popular theme song?

Answers on page 189.

## MAYA   (1967–1968, NBC)

1. Who played the two teenage leads, Terry Bowen and Raji?

2. Where was this series filmed?

3. What was Maya?

Answers on page 189.

## MOBILE ONE   (1975, ABC)

1. Who played Peter Campbell, and what was his profession?

2. What TV station did he work for?

Answers on page 189.

## THE NAME OF THE GAME   (1968–1971, NBC)

1. What connected the three characters in this unique rotating series?

2. Who played the three lead roles?

Answers on page 190.

## THE NANCY DREW MYSTERIES   (1977–1978, ABC)

1. Who played the title role of Nancy Drew?

2. Who was her father, who played him, and what was his profession?

3. Where did the Drews live?

4. Who played Nancy's friend George Fayne? (There were two.)

Answers on page 190.

## THE PERSUADERS   (1971–1972, ABC)

1. Who played the persuaders?
2. Who brought the persuaders together? How?

Answers on page 190.

## ROUTE 66   (1960–1964, CBS)

1. Who played the two lead roles in this series?
2. What type of car did the boys have?
3. Who took over as a lead character for the 1963–1964 season?

Answers on page 190.

## RUN FOR YOUR LIFE   (1965–1968, NBC)

1. Who played the lead role of Paul Bryan?
2. What was Paul Bryan's profession before he retired?
3. Why did Bryan retire?

Answers on page 190.

## SEA HUNT   (1957–1961; syndicated)

1. Who played ex-frogman Mike Nelson?
2. What was Nelson's new profession?
3. What was the name of Nelson's boat?

Answers on page 190.

## THE SIX MILLION DOLLAR MAN   (1974–1978, ABC)

1. Who was the Six Million Dollar Man, and what was his former profession?

2. What doctor performed the miracle surgery on the Six Million Dollar Man?

Answers on page 190.

## THE SWISS FAMILY ROBINSON   (1975–1976, ABC)

1. Who played Mr. and Mrs. Robinson, Karl and Lotte?

2. How many children did they have, and who played them?

3. What famous pirate character made a cameo appearance on the series?

Answers on page 190–191.

## T.H.E. CAT   (1966–1967, NBC)

1. What was T.H.E. Cat's real name?

2. What type of weapon did T.H.E. Cat carry?

3. At what nightclub did he maintain his office, and in what city?

Answers on page 191.

## TARZAN   (1966–1969, NBC and CBS)

1. Who played the lead role in this series?

2. Who played Jai, the orphan boy Tarzan became fond of?

Answers on page 191.

## THEN CAME BRONSON   (1969–1970, NBC)

1. Who played lead character Jim Bronson?

2. What caused Bronson to quit his job, hop on his motorcycle, and look for the meaning of life?

Answers on page 191.

## 240-ROBERT  (1979–1981, ABC)

1. There were three lead roles in this series. How many can you recall?

2. What agency did the three work for?

Answers on page 191.

Can you match the star of the series with the series title below? It's quite an adventure....

| | | |
|---|---|---|
| 1. | "Adventures of Robin Hood" (1955–58, CBS) | a. Tod Andrews |
| 2. | "Adventures of Sir Lancelot" (1956–67, NBC) | b. David McCallum |
| 3. | "Biff Baker, USA" (1952–53, CBS) | c. Dean Fredericks |
| 4. | "China Smith" (1952–55; syndicated) | d. William Russell |
| 5. | "Circus Boy" (1956–58, NBC and ABC) | e. Dan Duryea |
| 6. | "Gemini Man" (1976, NBC) | f. Barry Sullivan |
| 7. | "Gray Ghost" (1957; syndicated) | g. Ralph Taeger |
| 8. | "Harbourmaster" (1957–58, CBS and ABC) | h. Richard Greene |
| 9. | "Invisible Man" (1975–76, NBC) | i. Mickey Braddock |
| 10. | "Klondike" (1960–61, NBC) | j. Jon Hall |
| 11. | "Life and Times of Grizzly Adams" (1977–78, NBC) | k. Ben Murphy |
| 12. | "Ramar of the Jungle" (1952–56; syndicated) | l. Jock Mahoney |
| 13. | "Steve Canyon" (1958–60, NBC and ABC) | m. Alan Hale, Jr. |
| 14. | "Yancy Derringer" (1958–59, CBS) | n. Rich Moses |
| 15. | "Young Dan'l Boone" (1977, CBS) | o. Dan Haggerty |

Answers on page 191.

## MASTER QUIZ #1

### BATMAN (1968–1969, ABC)

In 1939, cartoonist Bob Kane introduced a new superhero to the world in *Detective Comics*. Almost thirty years later, most of Hollywood's major stars would be fighting for a chance to appear on the TV series based on Kane's character. This quiz is based on one of the most popular adventure series ever made. That's right! POW! THUMP!! CRACK!! THUD!! It's BATMAN!!

1. In what city did this series take place?

2. What was Batgirl's (1967–1968) name and occupation, and who played her?

3. What was the name of the house in which millionaire Bruce Wayne lived? What word was always used to describe it on the air?

4. What was Aunt Harriet's last name? Alfred the butler's?

5. How was the secret passage from the house to the Bat Cave activated?

6. What three actresses played the Catwoman?

7. What two actors played Mr. Freeze? The Riddler?

8. What happened to Bruce Wayne's parents?

9. What was Robin's real name?

10. Who played Commissioner Gordon? Chief O'Hara?

11. What color was the Batphone?

12. Who played the following roles?

| | |
|---|---|
| The Archer | Lola Lasagna |
| The Black Widow | Louie the Lilac |
| The Bookworm | The Mad Hatter |
| Egghead | The Penguin |

The Joker
King Tut

Shame
The Siren

Answers on pages 191–192.

## MASTER QUIZ #2

### SUPERMAN (1951–1957; syndicated)

Superman was created by Jerry Siegel and Joe Shuster in the 1930s and first appeared in comic-book form, then on radio, then on television.

Superman was a visitor to Earth from a strange planet. As the narrator told us at the opening of each episode, he had powers and abilities far beyond those of mortal men and fought a never-ending battle for truth, justice, and the American way.

In 1978, Superman became a big box-office hit as it was turned into a major motion picture. As we write this book, *Superman* the movie has given way to two sequels, and more may be coming.

So if you are one of those millions of people who have been following the man of steel for all these years, see how well you do on our Superman master quiz.

1. What was Superman's real name?

2. What planet did he come from?

3. What were the names of Superman's real parents?

4. The rocket that carried Superman to Earth landed in what town?

5. Name the couple that raised Superman after they discovered him in the rocket.

6. What was the pilot episode of the Superman series called?

7. What name did Superman take on earth, and for what newspaper did he work?

8. Who was the chief editor of this newspaper, and what was his famous phrase?

9. Name the two reporters on the newspaper who also became close friends of Superman.

10. What was the only thing that could harm Superman?

11. In the episode entitled "The Birthday Letter," what was the name of the little crippled girl, and where did she want Superman to take her?

12. What children's rhyme did the little girl's doll recite?

BONUS: Name the episode of "Superman" that was filmed but never shown on TV.

Answers on page 192.

# STOP IN THE NAME OF THE LAW!

IRED OF INJUSTICE? SICK OF SEEING THE guilty get away with just a slap on the wrist? Fed up with a system that treats the victim like a criminal? Well, have I got a program for you!

Through the years, the police drama has depicted a very broad border between right and wrong. And most often, if not always, by the end of any particular episode the guilty have been captured and punished and all is right with the world. Unfortunately, that is not exactly how things are in the real world, and this has been reflected in police dramas in recent years. But when television all began, and through the 1960s, the justice system was given many boosts per week through police dramas that showed how things should be instead of how they really were.

Television audiences didn't seem to mind this at all. Their sense of contentment with the system of justice needed to be reinforced on a regular basis, and that's exactly what the police drama did.

As we stated, as the years passed and reality slowly made its way into your television screens, things changed—not only in the police drama but in all forms of TV. Had TV been the first mode of communication to point out how things really were, there might have been a major problem, but luckily for television, viewers were already all too aware of how the real world worked, so they watched these "real" police dramas and found a strong association with them.

Association with leading characters was one of the major draws for audience approval in the police drama, probably even more so than the action within each episode. The programs showed their heroes as human beings instead of as supermen as the years went by. Because of this, a whole new audience got "hooked" on the police drama. We have reached a point now where personal relationships and realism seem to be the most important aspects of the police drama and the audience seems to be perpetuating itself.

Well, we've taken the precaution to set up a roadblock, so you have absolutely no way out. You might as well make the best of it and answer the following questions. Remember, anything you say might be held against you.

## ADAM 12 (1968–1975, NBC)

1. Who played Officer Pete Malloy, and who played Officer Jim Reed?

2. For what police department did they work?

3. Who was the producer of this TV show?

Answers on page 193.

## AMY PRENTISS (1974–1975, NBC)

1. Who played Amy Prentiss?

2. What police department did she work for, and what was her rank?

3. What was her husband's name and occupation?

Answers on page 193.

## BARETTA  (1975–1978, ABC)

1. The hotel where Baretta lived was run by what ex-cop? Who played him?

2. What was the theme song of "Baretta"?

Answers on page 193.

## THE BLUE KNIGHT  (1975–1976, CBS)

What was the real name of the Blue Knight, and who played him?

Answer on page 193.

## CADE'S COUNTY  (1971–1972, CBS)

1. Who played Sam Cade?

2. What was the setting for this Western/police drama?

3. One of the young deputies was played by the show's star's son. Who was he, and what was the name of his character?

Answers on page 193.

## CHIPS  (1977–1981, NBC)

1. What did "CHIPS" stand for?

2. Who were the two main stars of the show, and what characters did they play?

3. Name the police mechanic. Who played him?

Answers on page 193.

## CHOPPER ONE   (1974, ABC)

Name the two officers who patrolled their beat by way of a helicopter and tell who played them.

Answer on page 193.

## COLUMBO   (1971–1977, NBC)

1. Who played Columbo, and what was his ranking in the Los Angeles Police Department?

2. What was Columbo's famous trademark?

3. What was Columbo's first name?

Answers on page 194.

## DAN AUGUST   (1970–1971, ABC and CBS)

Who played Dan August, and what was his rank?

Answer on page 194.

## DELVECCHIO   (1976–1977, CBS)

1. Who played Delvecchio, and what city did he work out of?

2. Who played Delvecchio's partner and boss?

3. What was the name of Delvecchio's father, and what type of work did he do?

Answers on page 194.

## DRAGNET   (1952–1970, NBC)

1. Who portrayed Sgt. Joe Friday? How about his partner, Officer Bill Gannon?

2. Who was the director of "Dragnet"?

3. What was Sergeant Friday's badge number?

Answers on page 194.

## EISCHIED   (1979–1980, NBC)

1. Who played Eischied, and what city did he work out of?
2. Name Eischied's companion at home and at work.

Answers on page 194.

## THE F.B.I.   (1965–1974, ABC)

1. Name the character (full name) portrayed by Efrem Zimbalist, Jr.
2. Who was the assistant to the F.B.I. director?
3. Quinn Martin was the executive producer of this show, but who was the real force in getting this show to television?

Answers on page 194.

## HAWAII FIVE-O   (1968–1980, CBS)

1. Who played Detective Steve McGarrett?
2. Who played McGarrett's top assistant?
3. What was the name of the Governor of Hawaii?
4. Name Hawaii's most wanted man, who periodically gave McGarrett some of his more difficult times.

Answers on pages 194–195.

## HIGHWAY PATROL   (1955–1959; syndicated)

Who was the star of this police series?

Answer on page 195.

## IRONSIDE  (1967–1975, NBC)

1. Who played Ironside, and what was his rank in the police department?
2. Who played his bodyguard and aide?
3. How did Ironside become paralyzed?

Answers on page 195.

## JOE FORRESTER  (1975–1976, NBC)

Who played the role of Joe Forrester, and who played his girl friend?

Answer on page 195.

## KOJAK  (1973–1978, CBS)

1. Who played Kojak, and what was his rank?
2. What precinct did he work for?
3. What was Kojak's famous trademark?

Answers on page 195.

## LANIGAN'S RABBI  (1977, NBC)

Who played Lanigan, and what was the setting for this show?

Answer on page 195.

## M SQUAD  (1957–1960, NBC)

Who played the lieutenant, who also served as the narrator of this police show?

Answer on page 195.

## MADIGAN   (1972–1973, NBC)

Who played Madigan, and for what city did he work?

Answer on page 195.

## McCLOUD   (1970–1977, NBC)

1. Who played McCloud? Before coming to New York, he was the Deputy Marshall in what state?

2. What precinct in New York did he seldom work out of?

3. Who played McCloud's love interest? What was her occupation?

Answers on page 195.

## McMILLAN AND WIFE   (1971–1977, NBC)

1. Who played McMillan, and what was his occupation?

2. Who played his wife?

3. Who played the McMillans' maid?

Answers on page 196.

## THE MOD SQUAD   (1968–1973, ABC)

1. Name the three members that made up the Mod Squad.

2. Who was the captain that organized the Mod Squad?

3. Name the car they used to drive around in.

Answers on page 196.

## N.Y.P.D.   (1967–1969, ABC)

Who were the three main stars of the show?

Answer on page 196.

## NAKED CITY   (1958–1963, ABC)

What famous line was spoken every week on this show?

Answer on page 196.

## POLICE WOMAN   (1974–1978, NBC)

1. Who played Police Woman, and what was her character's name?
2. What division did she work for and in what city?

Answers on page 196.

## THE ROOKIES   (1972–1976, ABC)

1. Who played Officer Mike Danko, and who played his wife?
2. Who played Lieutenant Eddie Ryker?
3. What was the occupation of Mike Danko's wife?

Answers on page 196.

## S.W.A.T.   (1975–1976, ABC)

1. What did "SWAT" stand for?
2. Who was the commanding officer of SWAT, and who played him?

Answers on page 196.

## STARSKY AND HUTCH   (1975–1979, ABC)

1. Who played Starsky and Hutch?
2. Who played their boss?
3. What kind of car did they drive?

Answers on page 196.

## STREETS OF SAN FRANCISCO  (1972–1977 ABC)

1. Who played Detective Lieutenant Mike Stone, and for what police force did he work?

2. Name Detective Stone's two partners.

Answers on page 197.

## TOMA  (1973–1974, ABC)

1. Who played Toma, and what was the show based on?

2. Who played Toma's boss?

Answers on page 197.

## POLICE MATCHING # 1

Can you match the actor with the police drama series he or she starred in?

| | |
|---|---|
| 1. "The Asphalt Jungle" (1961, ABC) | a. Mitchell Ryan |
| 2. "Bert D'Angelo/ Superstar" (1976, ABC) | b. John Compton |
| 3. "Cain's Hundred" (1961–62, NBC) | c. Howard Duff |
| 4. "Caribe" (1975, ABC) | d. James Wainwright |
| 5. "Chase" (1973–74, NBC) | e. Paul Sorvino |
| 6. "City Detective" (1953–55; syndicated) | f. Teresa Graves |
| 7. "D.A.'s Man" (1959, NBC) | g. Peter Mark Richard |
| 8. "Dick Tracy" (1950–51, ABC) | h. Robert Lansing |
| 9. "87th Precinct" (1961–62, NBC) | i. Ralph Byrd |
| 10. "Felony Squad" (1966, ABC) | j. Stacy Keach |
| 11. "For the People" (1965, CBS) | k. Jack Warden |

12. "Get Christie Love"  l. William Shatner
  (1974–75, ABC)
13. "Harbor Command"  m. Clint Walker
  (1957–58; syndicated)
14. "Jigsaw" (1972–73, ABC) n. Wendell Corey
15. "Kodiak" (1974, ABC)  o. Rod Cameron

Answers on page 197.


## POLICE MATCHING # 2

You did so well last time, we're giving you another try. Match the star with his series. Good luck!

1. "The Lineup" (1954–60,  a. Jay Jostyn
  CBS)
2. "Man from Interpol"  b. Reed Hadley
  (1960, NBC)
3. "Manhunt" (1959–61;  c. Leslie Nielsen
  syndicated)
4. "Mr. District Attorney" d. James Earl Jones
  (1951–52, ABC)
5. "Most Wanted" (1976–77, e. David Birney
  ABC)
6. "Nakia" (1974, ABC)  f. Richard Wyler
7. "The New Breed"  g. Victor Jory
  (1961–62, ABC)
8. "O'Hara, U.S. Treasury" h. Ed Nelson
  (1971–72, CBS)
9. "Paris" (1979–80, CBS) i. David Janssen
10. "Racket Squad" (1957–59, j. Anthony Ross
  CBS)
11. "Sam" (1978, CBS)  k. Mark Harmon
12. "Serpico" (1976–77,  l. Warner Anderson
  NBC)
13. "The Silent Force"  m. Robert Forster
  (1970–71, ABC)
14. "The Telltale Clue" (1954, n. Mike Connors
  CBS)
15. "Tightrope"  o. Robert Stack
  (1959–60, CBS)

Answers on page 197.

## MASTER QUIZ

THE UNTOUCHABLES   (1959–1963, ABC)

"The Untouchables" was one of the most popular and violent police dramas ever produced. A week wouldn't pass without viewers witnessing one or more "bad guys" being riddled with bullets or worse. Seeing justice prevail in such an exaggerated way was probably what made the show so very popular. See how much you can recall about "The Untouchables."

1. Who was the narrator of this hit TV show?

2. Eliot Ness became a household name during and after this series run. Who played lawman Ness?

3. What real-life crime fighter was character Eliot Ness based on?

4. Who did the term "The Untouchables" refer to?

5. Who starred in the roles of the following bad guys? (a) Frank "The Enforcer" Nitti; (b) Jake "Greasy Thumb" Guzik; (c) Al Capone; (d) Bugs Moran; (e) Mad Dog Coll.

Answers on page 197.

# PUT THE WAGONS IN A CIRCLE!

**F**OR TWO DECADES THE WESTERN WAS ONE OF the most popular forms of television entertainment in existence. Perhaps it was because the Western could make a claim that was not quite true for any other type of television series airing at the time. The Western was truly American. It provided not only family entertainment but also an insight into American history. People seemed to be rather interested in how these early American pioneers expanded our nation into what it is today.

In the 1950s more than twenty-five Western series were launched by the networks, and the same was true in the 1960s. A great many of these were met with enthusiasm, and quite a few became very popular. However, in the 1970s only a dozen or so new Western series were attempted, and only two lasted more than two seasons, the majority of them falling by the wayside almost immediately.

There are a few reasons for this, and one may have been oversaturation. It is possible that America grew tired of the Western after so many series had been produced, but it is unlikely that this alone could have caused such a turnaround of opinion. We rather believe that attempts at a "newfangled" Western is what turned viewers off. The very reason why viewers found the Western unique, its simplicity and honesty, was being taken away in an attempt to make it more modern.

Well, viewers didn't want a "new" Western. They were content with the "old" Western, dealing with the Old West. Attempts at modernization were total failures as viewers turned instead toward the many innovations being offered on TV in the sexy seventies. Possibly their only link to the television of yesteryear was destroyed, and so was the standard of high quality that they had come to expect and appreciate.

We strongly feel that this refusal to leave well enough alone on the part of the television industry was a major catalyst in the decline of television programming since that time. Anyway, we must get back in the saddle and back on the trail, so here's a wagonload of questions for you to lasso. Git along now!

## BAT MASTERSON   (1959–1961, NBC)

1. Who played the lead role of Bat Masterson?

2. What two trademarks was Bat Masterson known for?

3. In what city did the series take place?

Answers on pages 197–198.

## THE BIG VALLEY   (1965–1969, ABC)

1. Who played the matriarch of the Barkley family?

2. There were four Barkley children. What were their names, and who played them?

Answers on page 198.

## BRANDED   (1965–1966, ABC)

1. The star of a popular 1950s Western series returned here to star as Jason McCord. Who was he?
2. From where did Jason McCord graduate?

Answers on page 198.

## BROKEN ARROW   (1956–1960, ABC)

1. Who was the chief of the Apache featured here? Who played him?
2. Who played the role of Indian Agent Tom Jeffords?

Answers on page 198.

## CHEYENNE   (1955–1963, ABC)

1. Who played the role of Cheyenne Brodie?
2. What was Cheyenne's sidekick's name during the first season?

Answers on page 198.

## CIMARRON STRIP   (1967–1971, CBS)

1. What was the Cimarron Strip?
2. Who played U.S. Marshal Jim Crown?

Answers on page 198.

## DANIEL BOONE   (1964–1970, NBC)

1. What actor played the title role of Daniel Boone?
2. Featured in the cast (1969–1970) was Gabe Cooper, a runaway slave. He was played by what football great?

Answers on page 198.

## DEATH VALLEY DAYS   (1952–1975; syndicated)

1. Can you name all five of the hosts that this series had during its long run?
2. Who was the major sponsor of the show?

Answers on page 198.

## HAVE GUN WILL TRAVEL   (1957–1963, CBS)

1. What was the featured character's name, and who played him?
2. What hotel did he stay in San Francisco?

Answers on page 198.

## HIGH CHAPARRAL   (1967–1971, NBC)

1. What was High Chapparal, and who owned it?
2. Who played Buck Cannon in this series?

Answers on page 199.

## HOTEL DE PAREE   (1959–1960, CBS)

1. Where was the Hotel De Paree?
2. Who played the lead role of Sundance?

Answers on page 199.

## THE LAWMAN   (1958–1962, ABC)

1. Who was the Lawman, and who played him?
2. Who played Deputy Johnny McKay?

Answers on page 199.

## THE LIFE AND LEGEND OF WYATT EARP (1955–1961, ABC)

1. Who played the title role of Wyatt Earp?
2. In this series, Bat Masterson was played by what actor?

Answers on page 199.

## THE LONE RANGER (1949–1957, ABC)

1. During this series's run there were two Lone Rangers. Name them both.
2. Who played the Indian sidekick, Tonto?

Answers on page 199.

## MAVERICK (1957–1962, ABC)

1. What were the Maverick brothers' first names, and who played them?
2. A major star who had his own series later in his career played Bart's best friend, Dandy Jim Buckley. Who was he?

Answers on page 199.

## THE MONROES (1966–1967, ABC)

1. This was a story about orphaned children on their own. How many were there?
2. How many of their names do you remember?

Answers on page 199.

## OVERLAND TRAIL (1960, NBC)

1. Who played Frederick Thomas Kelly in this series?

2. His partner, Frank Flippen, was played by what rugged actor?

Answers on page 199.

## RAWHIDE   (1959–1966, CBS)

1. What famous actor played the role of Rowdy Yates?
2. What was the trail boss's name, and who played him?

Answers on page 199.

## THE RIFLEMAN   (1958–1963, ABC)

1. What town was the setting for this very popular series?
2. Who played Lucas McCain? Who played Mark McCain? What was their relationship?

Answers on pages 199–200.

## SHANE   (1966, ABC)

1. Who played the lead role of Shane?
2. The series was based on the movie of the same name. What was the famous last line in the movie?

Answers on page 200.

## THE VIRGINIAN   (1962–1971, NBC)

1. Who played the Virginian?
2. What was the name of the ranch used as a setting in this series?

Answers on page 200.

## WAGON TRAIN   (1957–1965, NBC and ABC)

1. The series had two wagonmasters during its run. What were their names, and who played them?

2. From where did the wagon train always start?

Answers on page 200.

## WANTED: DEAD OR ALIVE   (1958–1961, CBS)

1. What famous actor played the role of Josh Randall?

2. Who played Josh's sidekick, Jason Nichols?

Answers on page 200.

## THE WILD, WILD WEST   (1965–1970, CBS)

1. James T. West was an undercover agent under what U.S. President?

2. Who played West, and who played his partner, Artemus Gordon?

3. What role did Michael Dunn, a dwarf, play?

Answers on page 200.

## ZORRO   (1957–1959, ABC)

1. What was Zorro's real name?

2. What actor played the title role?

3. What afflictions did his loyal companion, Bernardo, suffer from?

Answers on page 200.

After so much success in the fifties and sixties, the Western found itself in that terrible position in the ratings that every show tries to avoid. Within those ten years,

1970–1979, only two regularly scheduled series lasted for more than two seasons. Let's see if you remember them.


## ALIAS SMITH AND JONES   (1971–1973, ABC)

1. Due to an untimely death, two actors played the role of Hannibal Heyes (aka Joshua Smith). Can you name them?

2. Jed "Kid" Curry (aka Thadeus Jones) was played by what actor?

3. What actress played the role of Clementine Hale?

4. Before landing the co-starring role, the second Hannibal Heyes had what role in the series?

Answers on page 200.


## KUNG FU   (1972–1975, on ABC)

1. Who played the title role in "Kung Fu"?

2. What character did David Carradine play? Why was he in America?

3. Who were the two men who taught Carradine's character?

4. Carradine's character was often shown as a young boy. Who played that role?

Answers on pages 200–201.


## MATCHING # 1

Some things go together, like love and marriage, hot dogs and mustard, and cowboys and their sidekicks. Can you match the two up in the following quiz?

1.  "The Range Rider"              a. El Toro
    (1951–52; syndicated)

2. "Hopalong Cassidy"     b. Pancho
   (1949–51, NBC)
3. "Johnny Ringo" (1959–60,    c. Dick West
   CBS)
4. "The Cisco Kid" (1950–     d. Jingles
   56; syndicated)
5. "Kit Carson" (1951–55;     e. Red Connors
   syndicated)
6. "Wild Bill Hickok"      f. Cully
   (1951–58; syndicated)

Answers on page 201.

## MATCHING # 2

See if you can match the following Western series with its respective star.

1. "The Barbary Coast"     a. Wayne Maunder
   (1957–76, ABC)
2. "Black Saddle" (1959–60,   b. Ralph Taeger
   NBC, ABC)
3. "The Chisolms" (1979–80,   c. John Gavin
   CBS)
4. "Colt .45" (1957–60,     d. Robert Preston
   ABC)
5. "The Cowboys" (1974,     e. Tony Young
   ABC)
6. "Custer" (1967, ABC)     f. Jeanette Nolan
7. "The Dakotas" (1963,     g. James Arness
   ABC)
8. "Destry" (1964, ABC)     h. Doug McClure
9. "Dirty Sally" (1974, CBS)   i. Wayde Preston
10. "Dundee and the      j. Peter Breck
    Culhane" (1967, CBS)
11. "The Guns of Will     k. Walter Brennan
    Sonnett" (1967–69, ABC)
12. "Gunslinger" (1961, CBS)   l. Larry Ward
13. "Hondo" (1967, ABC)    m. Moses Gunn
14. "How the West Was    n. Dale Robertson
    Won" (1978–79, ABC)
15. "The Iron Horse" (1966–   o. John Mills
    68, ABC)

Answers on page 201.

## MATCHING #3

Here are some more popular Western series along with a list of the stars of those series. Can you match them up?

1. "Lancer" (1968–71, CBS)
2. "Laramie" (1959–63, NBC)
3. "Laredo" (1965–67, NBC)
4. "Law of Plainsman" (1959–62, NBC and ABC)
5. "MacKenzie's Raiders" (1958–59; syndicated)
6. "Man Without a Gun" (1957–59; syndicated)
7. "The Marshal of Gunsight Pass" (1950, ABC)
8. "Nichols" (1971–72, NBC)
9. "The Oregon Trail" (1977, NBC)
10. "The Outlaws" (1960–62, NBC)
11. "The Restless Gun" (1957–59, NBC)
12. "The Road West" (1966–67, NBC)
13. "Shotgun Slade" (1959–61; syndicated)
14. "Stoney Burke" (1962–63, ABC)
15. "Tombstone Territory" (1957–59, ABC)

a. Michael Ansara
b. Pat Conway
c. James Garner
d. Scott Brady
e. James Stacy
f. Russell Hayden
g. John Payne
h. Richard Carlson
i. John Smith
j. Barton MacLane
k. Rod Taylor
l. Rex Reason
m. Jack Lord
n. Barry Sullivan
o. Neville Brand

Answers on page 201.

## MASTER QUIZ

Although television Western series enjoyed great popularity in the 1950s and 1960s, there were two that stood out among the many well-accepted network entries. They, of course, were "Gunsmoke," which ran for an amazing

21 seasons, and "Bonanza," which ran for an incredible 14. It's unbelievable when you think about it. "Bonanza" was seemingly on forever and "Gunsmoke" was on seven years longer. Here's a master quiz based on these two classic series.

## GUNSMOKE (1955–1975, CBS)

1. What was the setting for the "Gunsmoke" series?

2. What was the name of Kitty Russell's saloon?

3. What was Doc Adams's first name? Who played him?

4. During the 21-year run this series enjoyed, Marshall Matt Dillon (James Arness) had two deputies, each for approximately ten years. Who were they, and who played them?

5. Who played the town blacksmith, half-Indian Quint Asper (1962–1965)?

Answers on page 201.

## BONANZA (1959–1973, NBC)

1. Who were the three Cartwright boys, and who played them?

2. What was the ranch cook's name, and who played him?

3. Candy, a wanderer, was hired as a ranch hand (1967–1970, 1972–1973). Who played Candy?

4. For a short while, reruns of "Bonanza" were being aired while the series was still in its original run, but were shown under a different title. What was it?

5. What was the title of the theme song from "Bonanza"?

Answers on page 201.

# STAKE-OUT!

N SOME WAYS YOU CAN LOOK AT THE DETEC-
tive drama as a variation of not one but two
other types of television series. The detective drama fea-
tures all the danger and excitement of the police drama
with a great measure of the glamor thrown in. The detective seems to get the better cases and so a chance to
mix with a better class of criminal. His undercover as-
signments usually lead to a fair share of romantic en-
counters and pleasurable situations. While performing the
same risky tasks as the police officer, the detective gets
the advantage of performing his job in much more exciting
surroundings.

Another way to view the detective drama is to see it
as the spy drama with a down-home flavor. As stated
earlier, the detective gets a chance to live a pretty exciting
existence, but unlike the spy drama, the series are basi-
cally set right here in the good old U.S.A., whereas most
of TV's spy dramas were set in Paris, Rome, London, or
some other equally exotic locale.

The great difference between one detective drama and
the next is the detective himself. In this section of the
book you will run into detectives ranging from handsome

virile men to sweet old ladies, with everything else in between represented. Offering this variety of detective heroes kept television audiences feeling that they were getting something new, and that was a smart ploy on the part of the networks.

Just remember as you attempt to crack the following questions that you should try and use all the cunning that our hero detectives would have used in cracking a particularly tough case. Now take this trivia interrogation and "make with some answers." And keep in mind that if you don't cooperate we have ways to make you talk!

## BANACEK   (1972–1974, NBC)

1. Who played the title role of Polish-American Thomas Banacek?

2. In what city did the series take place?

Answers on page 202.

## BANYON   (1972–1973, NBC)

1. How much would Banyon charge per day, for any and all cases?

2. Who played the role of Miles C. Banyon?

Answers on page 202.

## BRONK   (1975–1976, CBS)

1. Who played Bronk, and what was his full name?

2. In what city did the series take place?

3. How did Bronk's wife die?

Answers on page 202.

## BURKE'S LAW   (1963–1966, ABC)

1. Suave Captain Amos Burke was coolly played by what actor?

2. What was Burke's chauffeur's name, and what type of car did he drive?

3. To what was the title of this series changed?

Answers on page 202.

## CANNON   (1971–1976, CBS)

1. In what city did Frank Cannon practice his trade?

2. Who played the title role?

3. What type of car did Cannon drive?

Answers on page 202.

## CHARLIE'S ANGELS   (1977–1982, ABC)

1. Can you name the six angels and who played them?

2. Who was the voice of Charlie, and what was his last name?

3. What role did David Doyle play on this series?

Answers on page 202.

## CITY OF ANGELS   (1976, NBC)

1. Who played the lead role of Jake Axminster?

2. Marsha was his wacky secretary. Who played her?

Answers on page 202.

## COOL MILLION (1972–1973, NBC)

1. What was Jefferson Keyes's former occupation? Who played him?
2. Where did the title "Cool Million" come from?

Answers on page 202.

## FARADAY AND COMPANY (1973–1974, NBC)

1. For how many years was Frank Faraday wrongly held behind bars?
2. What was Frank's son's name, and who was his mother?

Answers on page 203.

## GRIFF (1973–1974, ABC)

1. Who played the title role of Wade Griffin?
2. What was the name of Griff's business?
3. How long was Griff a police officer?

Answers on page 203.

## HARRY-O (1974–1976, ABC)

1. What was Harry's last name? Who played him?
2. Harry moved from one city to another in 1975. Name them both.
3. Who played Harry's next-door neighbor?

Answers on page 203.

## HAWAIIAN EYE (1959–1963, ABC)

1. Who played the two leads, Tom Lopaka and Tracy Steele?

2. Where was their base of operations?

3. Who played singer-photographer Cricket Blake?

Answers on page 203.

## HONEY WEST   (1965–1966, ABC)

1. Who played Honey West?

2. Why was her lipstick unique?

3. Where was her office?

Answers on page 203.

## KAZ   (1978–1979, CBS)

1. What was Kaz's full name, and who played him?

2. What firm did Kaz work for?

3. Over what establishment did Kaz live?

4. Where did he earn his law degree?

Answers on page 203.

## LONGSTREET   (1971–1972, ABC)

1. Who played the role of Mike Longstreet, and what was his affliction?

2. What type of dog did Longstreet have? What was its name?

3. What else helped Longstreet get around?

4. Who played Longstreet's self-defense instructor in the series?

Answers on page 203.

## THE MANHUNTER   (1974–1975, CBS)

1. Who played Dave Barrett, the Manhunter?
2. In order to become a crime-fighter, Barrett had to give up his farm in what state?

Answers on page 204.

## MANNIX   (1967–1975, CBS)

1. Who played Joe Mannix, and what detective firm did he originally work for?
2. Who played the role of his loyal secretary, Peggy Fair?

Answers on page 204.

## MATT HELM   (1975–1976, ABC)

1. Who played the role that Dean Martin had made popular in the movies?
2. His sexy attorney and girl friend was played by what actress? What was her series name?

Answers on page 204.

## McCOY   (1975–1976, NBC)

1. What famous movie actor played the role of McCoy?
2. Who played McCoy's partner? What did he do for a living?

Answers on page 204.

## THE MOST DEADLY GAME   (1970–1971, ABC)

1. Three veteran actors starred in this series, all playing superior criminologists. Who played Jonathan Croft?

2. Who played Vanessa Smith? Mr. Arcane?

Answers on page 204.

## 77 SUNSET STRIP   (1958–1964, ABC)

1. The two lead characters were Stuart Bailey and Jeff Spencer (1958–1963). Who played these roles?
2. What nickname was character Gerald Lloyd Kookson III known by on the series?
3. What establishment was located next door to 77 Sunset Strip?

Answers on page 204.

## SHAFT   (1975–1974, CBS)

1. What handsome actor played the lead role of John Shaft?
2. Where did the series take place?
3. Ed Barth played Shaft's informer. What was his character's name?

Answers on page 204.

## THE SNOOP SISTERS   (1973–1974, NBC)

1. Who played the Snoop sisters, Ernesta and Gwen?
2. How did the Snoop sisters make their living?
3. What was Lieutenant Steve Ostrowski's relationship to the sisters? Who played him?

Answers on page 204.

## SWITCH   (1975–1978, CBS)

1. The two featured characters were an ex-cop and an ex-con. What were their names, and who played them?

2. What city was the setting for "Switch"?

3. Maggie was their secretary. Who played her?

Answers on page 205.

## TENAFLY (1973–1974, NBC)

1. Where did Harry Tenafly live? Who played him?

2. Ruth Tenafly, Harry's wife, was played by what actress?

Answers on page 205.

Can you match the series title with the actor who played the starring role? Give it a try!

| | | | |
|---|---|---|---|
| 1. | "Archer (1975, NBC) | a. | Kent Taylor |
| 2. | "Checkmate" (1960–62, CBS) | b. | Robert Conrad |
| 3. | "My Friend Tony" (1969, NBC) | c. | John Milton Kennedy |
| 4. | "The Duke" (1979, NBC) | d. | Anthony George |
| 5. | "Boston Blackie" (1951–53; syndicated) | e. | William Gargan |
| 6. | "Man in a Suitcase" (1968, ABC) | f. | Tom Conway |
| 7. | "Dear Detective" (1979, CBS) | g. | Brian Keith |
| 8. | "Armchair Detective" (1949, CBS) | h. | James Whitmore |
| 9. | "Mark Saber" (1957–60, ABC and NBC) | i. | Brenda Vaccaro |
| 10. | "Martin Kane, Private Eye" (1949–54, NBC) | j. | Richard Bradford |

Answers on page 000.

## MASTER QUIZ

THE THIN MAN   (1957–1959, CBS)

After enjoying great success in the movies with William Powell and Myrna Loy in the lead roles, "The Thin Man" came to television in 1957. It only lasted two seasons or so, but it was a good attempt at capturing the magic that the terrific movie series brought to American cinemagoers. Here is a small quiz to test how well you can remember television's attempt to reproduce movie magic.

1. Who played the starring roles of Nick and Nora Charles?

2. What type of dog was their pet canine, Asta?

3. Where did Nick and Nora Charles live?

4. Why was Asta more than just another dog?

5. What novelist created these characters?

6. What name did Nick's friend Beatrice Dane (1958–1959) use as an alias? Who played her?

Answers on page 205.

# Out of This World!

HERE SEEMS TO BE A SPECIAL FASCINATION with science fiction series on the part of television audiences. The science fiction series opened up a whole new frontier for the viewer. This is the seed from which most of the spectacular special effects we see in the movies today grew. Do you remember the spaceship in "Flash Gordon"? Guided by a wire, it flew with a lit firecracker acting as its booster rocket.

Special effects, however, were not the only attraction for TV viewers. Costumes, settings, and, of course, aliens from other planets were also major components of this science fiction TV magic.

Well, the following questions may not be strange if compared with some of our outer space alien friends, but they're far-out enough to keep you in orbit for a while.

BATTLESTAR GALACTICA    (1978–1980, ABC)

1. Who played Commander Adama, and his son, Captain Apollo?

2. What was the name of the half-robot, half-human villains?

3. After being cancelled after one season, the series came back the following season under what title?

Answers on page 205.

## BEYOND WESTWORLD   (1980, CBS)

What was Westworld?

Answer on page 205.

## BUCK ROGERS   (1950–1951, ABC)

1. Name the two actors who played Buck Rogers.

2. Who played Buck's campanion, Wilma Deering?

Answers on page 206.

## BUCK ROGERS IN THE 25TH CENTURY
(1979–1981, NBC)

1. Who played Captain William "Buck" Rogers?

2. Who played Dr. Huer?

3. Name the robot Dr. Huer gave to Buck Rogers.

Answers on page 206.

## FLASH GORDON   (1953–1954; syndicated)

1. Who played Flash Gordon?

2. Who played his two companions, Dale Arden and Dr. Zharkov?

3. What planet were Flash and his two friends headed for?

4. Who was the evil Emperor of this planet?

Answers on page 206.

## THE INVADERS  (1967–1968, ABC)

1. Who played David Vincent, the only human being to see the landing of a flying saucer?
2. What was David Vincent's occupation?
3. How did the viewers know which characters were aliens?

Answers on page 206.

## LOGAN'S RUN  (1977–1978, CBS)

1. Who played Logan?
2. What was the name of the community that Logan was running from?
3. Why was Logan running?

Answers on page 206.

## OUTER LIMITS  (1963–1965, ABC)

The beginning of each episode had your TV acting very strange, then you heard a voice telling you what was going on. What did it say?

Answer on page 206.

## PLANET OF THE APES  (1974, CBS)

1. Name the two astronauts who broke through the time barrier and found themselves on Earth, but in the far future.

2. Who played Galen, the chimpanzee who befriended the two astronauts?

Answers on pages 206–207.

## SPACE: 1999   (1975–1976; syndicated)

1. Who were the husband-and-wife team that played commander John Koenig and Dr. Helena Russell?

2. Who was Koenig's mentor, and who played him?

3. Who was the character that had the ability to transform herself into animal form and at times even plant life?

4. Moonbase Alpha was located on what planet?

Answers on page 207.

## STAR TREK   (1966–1969, NBC)

1. Name the two alien races that appeared throughout the three seasons that Star Trek aired.

2. Who played Captain James T. Kirk, and what was the name of the spaceship he was in command of?

3. Who played the chief engineer, and what was his nickname?

4. Who played the ship's doctor, and what was his nickname?

5. Who played Mr. Spock, and why was he known as a half-breed?

Answers on page 207.

## THE TWILIGHT ZONE   (1959–1965, CBS)

1. Who was the host of "The Twilight Zone"?

2. What was its memorable opening narration?

3. Name the episode that had no dialogue, and tell who starred in it.

4. In another episode, who played Mr. Death? (He is one of Hollywood's top leading men.)

5. In 1983 *Twilight Zone—the Movie* was released. Three of the four stories in the film were remakes from the TV series. Which ones were they?

Answers on page 207.

UFO   (1970; syndicated)

1. In what year does the show take place?

2. Shado was the name of the defense command center. What does it stand for?

3. Who was Shado's commander?

Answers on page 207.

MASTER QUIZ

Irwin Allen, who gave moviegoers some of the most spectacular disaster films of all time, gave TV viewers that same thrill for a number of seasons. So we now offer a special master quiz on these shows created by Irwin Allen, otherwise known as "the master of disaster."

We begin with "Voyage to the Bottom of the Sea," which was based on Irwin Allen's 1961 feature film of the same name. The TV series was quite different from the film, since many episodes dealt with giant sea creatures and aliens from other planets, but nevertheless it was always entertaining and became one of TV's all-time favorite series.

## VOYAGE TO THE BOTTOM OF THE SEA
(1964–1968, ABC)

1. What was the name of the atomic submarine used on the show as well as the minisub that was used periodically?

2. Who played Admiral Harriman Nelson?

3. Name the research center that Admiral Nelson was director of.

4. Who was the commander of the submarine?

5. Who was the Lieutenant Commander?

6. What was the name of the enemy submarine that appeared in the episode "The Lost Bomb"?

Answers on page 208.

We now look at "Lost in Space," another successful series by Irwin Allen. We go from the depths of the ocean floor to the vastness of outer space.

## LOST IN SPACE   (1965–1968, CBS)

1. What was the name of the family that got lost in space?

2. What was the name of the spacecraft they traveled in?

3. What was the title of the pilot episode?

4. In what year does the show take place?

5. The family became lost in space because of sabotage from a villainous stowaway. Who was he?

6. Who was the pilot of the spacecraft?

7. How many members made up this space-traveling family? Who played them?

8. Who supplied the voice of the robot?

Answers on page 208.

Irwin Allen then gave us "The Time Tunnel," about two young scientists who got suspended in time after entering an untested time tunnel. They found themselves moving from one point in history to another but were unable to get themselves back home. The show only lasted one season, but it was very popular in reruns in the years to follow.

## THE TIME TUNNEL (1966–1967, ABC)

1. Name the two scientists who entered the time tunnel.

2. When they first entered the time tunnel, where did they find themselves in history?

3. Name the two associates that worked each week to get the two scientists back home.

4. In what state was the time tunnel located?

5. Name the episode in which one of the scientists goes back home, meets his father, and confronts himself as a child.

Answers on page 208.

Our last show in this master quiz is "Land of the Giants," a little more of a fantasy than Irwin Allen's other three shows. It dealt with the exploits of seven people trapped in a strange world inhabited by giants.

## LAND OF THE GIANTS (1968–1970, ABC)

1. In what year does the show take place?

2. What was the original destination of the spaceship before it entered the space warp?

3. What was the name of the spaceship?

4. Who were the pilot and co-pilot?

5. What was the title of the first episode?

Answers on pages 208–209.

# WHICH WAY TO THE FRONT?

THERE WEREN'T ALL THAT MANY WAR DRAMAS, produced for television in the fifties, sixties, and seventies, but the few that were done attempted to offset their scarcity with a truckload of action scenes in each episode.

Viewers were impressed with the inclusion of actual battle footage in almost every episode, feeling that it added a true sense of realism to the particular program. The real reason actual footage was used was probably to cut down production costs. Rather than hiring four thousand extras to run around shooting each other, a network could simply dig through their file footage until they found a battle that would suffice.

Characters on war drama series were shown in two distinctly different lights. First, of course, there were the battle situations, where they could display their clear-mindedness and leadership qualities, their acceptance of a bad situation, and their courage in making the best of that situation. They, however, were also shown as all-around good guys, not so much in the sense of "good vs. evil" but in the sense of "Gee, what a nice fellow he is." Television gave its heroes a human quality that stuck in your mind even as you watched them in mortal combat. For the first time, viewers who had never fought in a war could really associate with these characters and gain some sense, however small, of the human aspect of war, the idea that a war may be made up of armies, but armies are made up of men.

If you are courageous enough to enter the battle zone, continue on and take the challenge that the following questions have in store.

## THE AMERICANS   (1961, NBC)

1. What war did this series deal with?

2. The series dealt with two brothers. What were their names?

3. Where did the brothers grow up?

Answers on page 209.

## BAA BAA BLACK SHEEP   (1976–1978, NBC)

1. Who did our friend Robert Conrad portray in yet another series?

2. After initial cancellation, this series reappeared under what title?

3. Who played Colonel Lord, USMC, and Captain Gutterman (1976–77)?

Answers on page 209.

## COMBAT   (1962–1967, ABC)

1. The two major characters were Lieutenant Gil Hanley and Sergeant Chip Saunders. Who played these roles?

2. Where did the fighting take place?

3. Who played platoon comic Private Braddock (1962–63)?

Answers on page 209.

## COMBAT SERGEANT   (1956, ABC)

1. Who played Combat Sergeant Nelson?
2. Where was this series set?

Answers on page 209.

## CONVOY   (1965, NBC)

1. Who played Commander Dan Talbot?
2. What ship was Talbot stationed on?
3. What was the name of the merchant freighter run by Captain Ben Foster?

Answers on page 209.

## FROM HERE TO ETERNITY   (1979–1980, NBC)

1. Where was this series set? When?
2. Two actresses played Karen Holmes. Who were they?
3. What television science fiction series star played Major Dana Holmes?

Answers on page 209.

## THE GALLANT MEN   (1962–1963, ABC)

1. What country was the setting for this war-action series?
2. What infantry division's actions were chronicled here?

Answers on page 209.

## JERICHO   (1966–1967, CBS)

For what country and what agency did the three lead characters work? a. Franklin Shepard (Don Francks), b. Jean-Gaston Andre (Marino Mase), c. Nicholas Gage (John Leyton)

Answer on page 210.

## O.S.S.   (1957–1958, ABC)

1. What was the O.S.S.?
2. What real-life agency replaced the O.S.S.?
3. Who starred as "The Chief"?

Answers on page 210.

## ONCE AN EAGLE   (1976–1977, NBC)

1. What war was the time setting for this series?
2. Who played the two leads in this series?

Answers on page 210.

## THE RAT PATROL   (1966–1968, ABC)

1. Where was this series set?
2. Where was the series actually filmed?
3. Who were the four rat-patrollers?
4. What vehicles did they use?

Answers on page 210.

## TWELVE O'CLOCK HIGH   (1964–1967, ABC)

1. Who played Brigadier General Frank Savage (1964–65)?

2. When Savage was killed on a mission, who took over command?

3. What group did they command?

Answers on page 210.

## THE WACKIEST SHIP IN THE ARMY (1965–1966, NBC)

1. What was the wackiest ship in the army?

2. What was the name of the ship?

3. Major Simon Butcher and Lieutenant Richard "Rip" Riddle "flip-flopped" command of the ship. Who played these roles?

Answers on page 210.

## MASTER QUIZ

Many of television's war dramas developed somewhat of a cult following. One of these series was on for only a year, but it featured a likeable group of men who sought danger and always came away with another roaring success. If you've been through basic training, maybe you can answer the following questions.

## GARRISON'S GORILLAS (1967–1968, ABC)

1. Where did the army get Garrison's gorillas?

2. During what war did this series take place?

3. Why did Garrison's gorillas agree to fight against the Germans?

4. What were the nicknames of the four lead characters?

5. Who played Lieutenant Craig Garrison?

6. What country served as a base for Garrison's gorillas?

Answers on pages 210–211.

# GENERALLY
# SPEAKING . . .

**C**ERTAIN TELEVISION SERIES DON'T FALL INTO any specific category. Instead, they drift into many different categories. Some share their time between comedy and drama. Others mix suspense with adventure; but whatever the combination, they have been a popular source of entertainment for television audiences for many years.

Although not quite episodic or serialized enough to compare with today's prime-time soap operas, they nevertheless present a feeling of continuity to which viewers could easily get addicted.

On the following pages you will find questions on more than thirty of all these encompassing series. Generally speaking, we're sure you'll do just fine.

## APPLE'S WAY   (1974–1975, CBS)

1. What city was the setting for this series?

2. Who played George Apple and what was his profession?

3. From where did the Apples move?

4. What two child actors played Patricia Apple?

5. Who played Paul Apple's "older woman" crush object in one episode?

Answers on page 211.

## BRACKEN'S WORLD (1969–1970, NBC)

1. For what company did many of the main characters work?

2. Two actors played John Bracken, company head, yet their roles were very different. Why is this so and who were the actors involved?

Answers on page 211.

## CORONET BLUE (1967, CBS)

Who played Michael Alden, and what was he in search of?

Answer on page 211.

## EIGHT IS ENOUGH (1977–1981, ABC)

1. How many of the Bradford children can you name?

2. What newspaper did Tom Bradford write for?

3. What actress played Tom's wife in the first few episodes?

4. At what school did Tom's second wife, Abby, teach? Who played her?

Answers on page 211.

# EMERGENCY   (1972–1977, NBC)

1. Whose actions did this series chronicle?
2. Who played John Gage and Roy De Soto?
3. What animated series was a spinoff of "Emergency"?

Answers on page 211.

# FAMILY   (1976–1980, ABC)

1. Where did the Lawrence family live?
2. "Buddy" Lawrence was played by Kristy McNichol. What was "Buddy's" real name?
3. Who played Doug Lawrence? What was his profession?

Answers on pages 211–212.

# THE FAMILY HOLVAK   (1975–1977, NBC and CBS)

1. Who played Tom Holvak? What was his profession?
2. What accomplished actress played Elizabeth Holvak?

Answers on page 212.

# HENNESEY   (1959–1962, CBS)

1. Who played "Chick" Hennesey?
2. The naval base at which he was stationed was located in what city?
3. Who played nurse Martha Hale, Hennesey's romantic interest?

Answers on page 212.

## HERE COME THE BRIDES   (1968–1970, ABC)

1. Who played the three Bolt brothers?
2. Where did the Bolts find prospective brides to accompany them back to Seattle?
3. Who played the roles of Lottie Hatfield and Captain Charley Clancy?
4. What did the Bolts do for a living?

Answers on page 212.

## KOLCHAK: THE NIGHT STALKER   (1974–1975, ABC)

1. Carl Kolchak (Darren McGavin) was a reporter for whom?
2. Who played Kolchak's editor, Tony Vincenzo?

Answers on page 212.

## THE LONG, HOT SUMMER   (1965–1966, ABC)

1. Where did this series take place?
2. Who owned the town? What two actors played the role during the series's run?
3. Who played the role of Ben Quick?

Answers on page 212.

## LUCAS TANNER   (1974–1975, NBC)

1. Lucas Tanner was played by what actor?
2. Where did he teach and in what city was the school?
3. Who played Tanner's little boy neighbor, Glendon?

Answers on page 212.

## MR. NOVAK  (1963–1965, NBC)

1. Who played the lead role?
2. At what school did he teach?
3. Who played Martin Woodridge, principal of the school (1964–1965)?

Answers on page 212.

## THE PAPER CHASE  (1978–1979, CBS)

1. What character did John Houseman play?
2. Who played James T. Hart, and where did he work part-time?
3. At what school was the series filmed?

Answers on page 213.

## PEYTON PLACE  (1964–1969, ABC)

1. Where was Peyton Place?
2. Matthew Swain (Wayne Anderson) was the editor of what publication?
3. What role did Mia Farrow play?

Answers on page 213.

## ROOM 222  (1969–1974, ABC)

1. At what school did this series take place?
2. Who played principal Seymour Kaufman?
3. What subject did Alice Johnson (Karen Valentine) teach?
4. Who played Pete Dixon? Liz McIntyre?

Answers on page 213.

## SAN FRANCISCO INTERNATIONAL AIRPORT (1970–1971, NBC)

1. Who played the role of airport manager Jim Conrad?
2. Who played the chief of airport security Bob Hatten?

Answers on page 213.

## SARGE (1971–1972, NBC)

1. "Sarge" was his nickname, but who was he?
2. At what parish did he serve?
3. Why was he called "Sarge"?

Answers on page 213.

## SKAG (1980, NBC)

1. What was Skag's full name, who played him, and what was his profession?
2. In what city did the series take place?
3. Who played Jo, Skag's wife?

Answers on page 213.

## THE SMITH FAMILY (1971–1972, ABC)

1. Who played Detective Sergeant Chad Smith?
2. Where did daughter Cindy go to school? Who played her?
3. Who played son Bob Smith?
4. What was the theme song from this series?

Answers on page 213.

## THE WALTONS   (1972–1979, CBS)

1. What was the name of the local paper published by John-Boy?

2. Who did Mary Ellen marry? How did he eventually die?

3. Who played the Baldwin sisters?

Answers on page 214.

## THE WHITE SHADOW   (1978–1981, CBS)

1. At what school did Ken Reeves coach basketball? Who played him?

2. What pro team had Reeves supposedly played for?

3. In 1980, what championship did Reeves's team win?

Answers on page 214.

Here's a list of some other general drama series to appear on television. Can you match the series with its star?

| | | |
|---|---|---|
| 1. | "Beacon Hill" (1975, CBS) | a. Mitchell Ryan |
| 2. | "Court-Martial" (1966, ABC) | b. Andy Griffith |
| 3. | "Executive Suite" (1976–77, CBS) | c. Bert Kramer |
| 4. | "The Fitzpatricks" (1977–78, CBS) | d. Anthony Quinn |
| 5. | "Gibbsville" (1976, NBC) | e. Pamela Bellwood |
| 6. | "Headmaster" (1970–71, CBS) | f. Charles Bronson |
| 7. | "James at 15" (1977–78, NBC) | g. David Dukes |

8. "Man and the City"
   (1971–72, ABC)                    h. John Savage

9. "Man with a Camera"              i. Craig Stevens
   (1958–60, ABC)

10. "Mr. Broadway"                   j. Bradford Dillman
    (1964, CBS)

11. "Sixth Sense"                    k. Gary Collins
    (1972, ABC)

12. "W.E.B." (1978, NBC)             i. Lance Kerwin

Answers on page 214.

## MASTER QUIZ

### THE FUGITIVE   (1963–1967, ABC)

"The Fugitive" was the story of an innocent man on the run from the law. The man, Dr. Richard Kimble, had been convicted for the murder of his wife, a crime he did not commit. A one-armed man was seen leaving the scene of the crime by Kimble, but he was unable to prove this to the police.

As he was being transported to prison, certain happenings led to his escape and so he began his search for the real killer (the one-armed man), with Lieutenant Gerard constantly on his tracks.

For the next few seasons, TV viewers watched as Richard Kimble kept hot on the trail of the one-armed man while always managing to keep two steps ahead of the persistent Lieutenant Gerard. He wanted desperately to set the record straight by catching the real killer so he could finally stop running. The day finally came, on the night of Tuesday, August 29, 1967, when viewers watched as Richard Kimble at last confronted the one-armed man, exonerating himself. We now offer this master quiz on this award-winning series.

1. Who played the role of the fugitive, Dr. Richard Kimble?

2. What was the name of Richard Kimble's wife, and who played her?

3. Who was the narrator that kept viewers aware of Richard Kimble's situation?

4. How did Richard Kimble escape as he was being sent to prison?

5. In the episode "The Girl from Little Egypt" we are shown the murder trial of Dr. Kimble through flashbacks. What were his last words before the judge passed sentence on him?

6. What was the verdict and sentence in the trial?

7. How many years did his search last?

8. What was the name of the two-part episode that ended the running of Richard Kimble?

9. What was the date of the murder of Richard Kimble's wife?

10. Who was in the house the night that Mrs. Kimble was killed, but kept quiet until the final episode?

11. Who played Richard Kimble's sister, Donna Taft?

12. What was Richard Kimble's brother-in-law's name and who played him?

13. On what date did the running stop for Richard Kimble?

Bonus: Name the city and state where Richard Kimble lived before he started running.

# STOP THE PRESSES!

**T**HIS SECTION OF THE BOOK CONCERNS ITSELF with something of television oddity. You would think that newspaper dramas, that is, dramas based on characters involved with the newsprint industry (reporters, editors, et al), wouldn't be that numerous. In fact, there have been well over a dozen, which is amazing when you consider the limits you are bound by. It would be like producing twelve series about ice cream men. I mean, after a while, they all look alike, right? But somehow television managed to come up with a new angle for each of these programs.

The fact that none of these series ever really made it big does not stop the newspaper drama from popping up on the television schedule on a rather regular basis. The explanation here is hard to come by. There may be a special association the audience feels with these characters since they are involved in keeping us informed about everything that's going on in the world around us.

Whatever the reason, we were amazed to come across so many of this type of drama, so we dedicated an entire section to them. See how many of the following quizzes you can pass.

## THE ANDROS TARGETS   (1977, CBS)

1. Who played Mike Andros?
2. In what city did the series take place?

Answers on page 215.

## BIG TOWN   (1950–1956, CBS, DUMONT, and NBC)

1. What was the lead character's name on "Big Town"?
2. During its seven-year existence, one character, that of Lorelei Kilbourne, was played by more than one actress. How many actresses played the part during the series's run?

Answers on page 215.

## CRIME PHOTOGRAPHER   (1951–1952, CBS)

1. Casey, the lead character, was played by two actors. Who where they?
2. What was Casey's hangout?
3. What trio performed at Casey's favorite club?

Answers on page 215.

## THE FRONT PAGE   (1949–1950, CBS)

1. What jobs did Walter Burns and Hildy Johnson hold at the paper?
2. What was unique about the actor playing Walter Burns?

Answers on page 215.

## FRONT PAGE DETECTIVE   (1951–1953, DUMONT)

1. Who played the lead role of David Chase?

2. What was David's girl friend's occupation?

Answers on page 215.

## I COVER TIMES SQUARE   (1950–1951, ABC)

1. Who played Johnny Warren?
2. Where did Warren hang out?

Answers on page 215.

## KINGSTON: CONFIDENTIAL   (1977, NBC)

1. Raymond Burr was R. B. Kingston, a top executive of what prominent communications network? Where was it located?
2. Who played Jessica Frazier, the network's operating officer?

Answers on page 215.

## LOU GRANT   (1977–1980, CBS)

1. Who owned the paper Lou Grant worked for?
2. Who was the managing editor of the paper?

Answers on page 215.

## NOT FOR PUBLICATION   (1951–1952, DUMONT)

The lead character, a reporter, was named Collins. During this series run, two actors played him. Who were they?

Answer on page 216.

## THE REPORTER   (1964, CBS)

1. Who played Danny Taylor, reporter and lead character in this series?

2. Artie Burns was played by George O'Hanlon. What was his occupation?

Answers on page 216.

## THE ROARING TWENTIES   (1960–1962, ABC)

1. There were two lead characters, both reporters, in this series. Who were they, and who played them?
2. At what speakeasy were the two lead characters often found?
3. Who was the singer in the speakeasy?

Answers on page 216.

## SAINTS AND SINNERS   (1962–1963, NBC)

Who played the roles of Nick Alexander, a reporter, and Lizzie Hogan, a Washington correspondent?

Answer on page 216.

## TARGET: THE CORRUPTORS   (1956–1959, ABC)

Name the investigative reporter and the undercover agent featured on this series.

Answer on page 216.

## WIRE SERVICE   (1956–1959, ABC)

1. What wire service was featured in this series?
2. What title was this series known by in reruns?
3. Who played Katherine Wells, reporter?

Answers on page 216.

Below you will find a list of some of the newspaper dramas featured in this section. Can you match the series title with the name of the newspaper featured on that series? Good luck!

1. "The Andros Targets" (1977, CBS)
2. "Big Town" (1950–56, CBS, Dumont, and NBC)
3. "Crime Photographer" (1951–52, CBS)
4. "The Front Page" (1949–50, CBS)
5. "Lou Grant" (1977–80, CBS)
6. "Not For Publication" (1951–52, Dumont)
7. "The Reporter" (1964, CBS)
8. "The Roaring Twenties" (1960–62, ABC)
9. "Saints and Sinners" (1962–63, NBC)

a. Morning Express
b. New York Globe
c. The Ledger
d. Illustrated Press
e. New York Forum
f. Center City Examiner
g. New York Bulletin
h. L.A. Tribune
i. New York Record

Answers on page 216.

# MAKE 'EM LAUGH!

**I**T WILL PROBABLY NOT SURPRISE YOU WHEN we state that the situation comedy is, by far and away, the most popular form of television entertainment ever to pass through your TV tubes. There have been more situation comedies, or sitcoms, produced for television than any other type of series, and by a very large margin. It stands to reason, then, that there have been more classic sitcoms than any other type of program. People will invariably alter personal schedules so that they will be able to watch their favorite sitcoms on TV!

People—and this is not strictly referring to television-watchers—love to laugh! That is an obvious statement of fact. Through the sitcom, we have been afforded an endless parade of priceless moments that have lodged themselves in the deepest recesses of our minds. We tend to draw from these memories when a real-life parallel arises. After going through a particularly rough day at work, one might think back to the horrible day Lucy and Ethel had at the candy factory wrapping chocolates. The possibilities are as endless as the joy we have received through the sitcom itself.

Popularity is the most important result for any TV

program, and the sitcom has had the greatest success in this area because of a built-in enticement to prospective viewers. You tune in because you want to laugh! Other series offer many different things to the viewer. Adventure if you're in the mood. Intrigue or suspense, if that's what you desire, but we always seem to crave laughter. The sitcom affords us a reason to laugh, and in today's world we can always use a reason to laugh.

Not only comedians have starred in this most popular form of television entertainment. Because of the tremendous audience response a winning sitcom receives, entertainers from other areas have been tempted to try their hand at the sitcom, some with success, most without. Serious actors have tried. Sports figures have tried. Singers have tried. Almost everyone has tried at one time or another.

There seems to be no set pattern as to which sitcoms make it and which don't. More new sitcoms are aired every season and more sitcoms fail every season, and every once in a while one sticks, and out of every hundred that stick, one just might establish its place in television history and become known as a classic. The classic sitcom is the most talked about, most remembered, and most endearing of all forms of television entertainment. On the following pages we offer master quizzes on some of them.

Because of the incredibly large number of sitcoms that have been produced for television and because of our desire to include as many of them as we possibly could into this book, we have dedicated three separate sections to the TV sitcom.

The first section deals with sitcoms of the 1950s. The second section will quiz you on sitcoms of the 1960s, the decade that has given us so many fond memories. The final section will contain questions on sitcoms of the 1970s. We feel that there is a sincere effort underfoot to try and recapture the magic of the 1950s and 60s in sitcoms today, but so far, it is failing rather miserably, so we will journey back to a magical time when we rushed home to watch our favorites and talked about them for a whole week until the next episode was televised.

# THE ABBOTT & COSTELLO SHOW
(1951–1953; syndicated)

1. Who owned the house that the boys lived in?
2. What coffee shop was down the block from the boys' house?
3. Who played the roles of Mike the Cop, Mr. Bacciagalupe, and Stinky?

Answers on page 216.

# THE ADVENTURES OF OZZIE & HARRIET
(1952–1966, ABC)

1. Who produced this series?
2. Where did David Nelson work part-time?

Answers on page 217.

# AMOS 'N' ANDY   (1951–1953, CBS)

1. Who played the two title roles in this series?
2. Where was the series set?
3. Character George Stevens was the head of what Lodge? What was his nickname?
4. What was Amos's occupation?
5. What was Andy's girl friend's name?

Answers on page 217.

# THE ANN SOTHERN SHOW   (1958–1961, CBS)

1. What did Ann's character, Katy O'Connor, do for a living?
2. Who was Katy's best friend?

3. Katy's best friend fell in love with a dentist. What was his name, and who played him?

Answers on page 217.

## BACHELOR FATHER   (1957–1962, CBS, NBC, and ABC)

1. What was Bentley Gregg's occupation?

2. Who played houseboy Peter Tong?

3. What was Peter's cousin's name?

4. Linda Evans appeared in one episode under what other name?

Answers on page 217.

## BLONDIE   (1957 and 1969, NBC and CBS)

1. Who was Dagwood's boss?

2. There were two productions of this series. Both ran for one season each. The first, in 1957, starred whom as Mr. and Mrs. Bumstead?

3. Who played Mr. and Mrs. Bumstead in the second series (1969)?

4. What was their dog's name? How about their kids?

Answers on page 217.

## THE BOB CUMMINGS SHOW   (1955–1959, NBC and CBS)

1. Under what other title was this series aired?

2. What was Bob Collin's occupation?

3. Who played Bob's widowed sister, Margaret Mac-Donald?

Answers on page 217.

## THE DANNY THOMAS SHOW  (1953–1971, ABC and CBS)

1. During the first three seasons, this series was known as what?
2. What was Danny's occupation?
3. In 1970, the series returned under what title?
4. Who played Charlie and Bunny Halper?
5. Linda Williams was played by the same actress in both runs of this series. Who was she?

Answers on page 218.

## DECEMBER BRIDE  (1954–1961, CBS)

1. Who played lead character Lily Ruskin?
2. What was everyone always trying to do for Lily?

Answers on page 218.

## DENNIS THE MENACE  (1959–1963, CBS)

1. Who drew the cartoon "Dennis the Menace"?
2. Where did Dennis live?
3. Who was Dennis's neighbor? Who played him? (There were two!)
4. What was the neighbor's hobby?
5. What was the neighbor's dog's name?

Answers on page 218.

## THE DONNA REED SHOW  (1968–1966, ABC)

1. Where did the Stones live?
2. What was Alex Stone's occupation? Who played him?

3. What number-one song was introduced on this series? Who sang it?

Answers on page 218.

## FATHER KNOWS BEST (1954–1963, CBS, NBC, and ABC)

1. What was Jim Anderson's occupation? Who did he work for?

2. What were daughter Kathy's, daughter Betty's, and son James Junior's nicknames?

3. Where did the Andersons live?

4. Who played lovely Margaret Anderson, Jim's wife?

Answers on page 218.

## FIBBER McGEE AND MOLLY (1959–1960, NBC)

1. What was the McGees' address?

2. What two things was Fibber McGee most known for?

Answers on page 218.

## THE GALE STORM SHOW (1956–1960, CBS, ABC)

1. What was Susanna Pomeroy's occupation?

2. Who was Susanna's best friend? Who played her?

Answers on page 218.

## THE GEORGE BURNS AND GRACIE ALLEN SHOW (1950–1958, CBS)

1. Who were the Burns's neighbors?

2. Bea Benaderet played the female half of the neighbor couple, but her husband was played by four actors from 1950 to 1958. Can you name them?

3. In what city was this series produced?

Answers on page 219.

## THE GOLDBERGS (1949–1954, CBS, NBC, and DU-MONT)

1. What was the Goldbergs' address?
2. Three actors played the role of Jake Goldberg from 1949 to 1954. Can you name them?

Answers on page 219.

## THE GREAT GILDERSLEEVE (1955, NBC)

1. What was the Great Gildersleeve's full name, and who played him?
2. What was Gildersleeve's profession?
3. Who played Gildersleeve's two wards, Leroy and Marjorie?

Answers on page 219.

## I MARRIED JOAN (1952–1955, NBC)

1. Who was Joan's husband? His occupation?
2. Who played Joan?

Answers on page 219.

## LEAVE IT TO BEAVER (1957–1963, CBS and ABC)

1. Where did the Cleavers live?
2. Who were Beaver's schoolteachers?
3. Two of the Beaver's closest friends were Larry and Whitey. What were their last names?

4. Wally's two best buddies were "Lumpy" and Eddie Haskell. Who played them?

Answers on page 219.

## THE LIFE OF RILEY   (1949–1958, NBC)

1. Who played Mr. and Mrs. Chester A. Riley in the 1949–1950 series? How about the 1953–1958 series?
2. Where did Riley work?
3. What was Riley's famous phrase?

Answers on page 219.

## LIFE WITH FATHER   (1953–1955, CBS)

1. What city was the setting for this series?
2. Who was "father"?

Answers on page 219.

## MAMA   (1949–1954, CBS)

1. How did the show begin each week?
2. What was "Papa" Lars Hansen's occupation? Who played him?
3. What famous stage actress beautifully played the title role of "Mama" Marta Hansen?

Answers on page 220.

## THE MANY LOVES OF DOBIE GILLIS   (1959–1963, CBS)

1. Where did Dobie live?
2. What were his parents' names? Who played them?

3. Who was Dobie's beatnik friend? His heartthrob?

Answers on page 220.

## MR. PEEPERS   (1952–1955, NBC)

1. Where did Mr. Peepers teach science?

2. What was Mr. Peepers' first name?

3. Who played Mr. Peepers' best friend, Harvey Weskit? What subject did he teach?

Answers on page 220.

## MY FRIEND IRMA   (1952–1954, CBS)

1. What was Irma Peterson's occupation?

2. Where did Irma live and with whom?

3. What well-known actress played Irma's boss's wife, Mrs. Richard Rhinelander?

Answers on page 220.

## MY LITTLE MARGIE   (1952–1955, CBS, NBC)

1. Where did Margie's dad, Vernon Albright, work?

2. Where did Margie live, and with whom?

3. What was Margie's boyfriend's name?

Answers on page 220.

## OUR MISS BROOKS   (1952–1956, CBS)

1. Where did Miss Connie Brooks teach English?

2. What man was Miss Brooks always trying to hook?

3. Upon leaving the school at which she first taught, where did Miss Brooks find a job?

Answers on page 220.

## THE PEOPLE'S CHOICE   (1955–1958, ABC)

1. What character did Jackie Cooper play?
2. What job did he get after graduating from law school?
3. Who did he marry?

Answers on page 220.

## THE PHIL SILVERS SHOW   (1955–1959, CBS)

1. What was the setting for this series?
2. What was the original title of this series?
3. What platoon did Sergeant Ernie Bilko command?

Answers on page 221.

## THE REAL McCOYS   (1957–1963, ABC, CBS)

1. The McCoys moved from what state to what other state?
2. What was the farmhand's name? Who played him?
3. What was the rerun title for this series?
4. Who played the roles of Luke and Kate McCoy?

Answers on page 221.

## TOPPER   (1953–1956, CBS, ABC, NBC)

1. Why were Marion and George Kirby and their dog unique?

2. Who owned the house they returned to? Who played him?

Answers on page 221.

Can you match the star with the 1950s situation comedy they appeared in? This is a tough one, so we wish you good luck!

| | | |
|---|---|---|
| 1. | "Beulah" (1950–53, ABC) | a. Stubby Kaye |
| 2. | "Boss Lady" (1952, NBC) | b. Lugene Sanders |
| 3. | "The Brothers" (1956–58, CBS) | c. William Demarest |
| 4. | "Heaven for Betsy" (1952, CBS) | d. Lynn Bari |
| 5. | "Jamie" (1953–54, ABC) | e. Buddy Hackett |
| 6. | "Love & Marriage" (1959–60, NBC) | f. Gale Gordon |
| 7. | "The Marriage" (1954, NBC) | g. Elena Verdugo |
| 8. | "Meet Corliss Archer" (1951–52, CBS) | h. Brandon DeWilde |
| 9. | "Meet Millie" (1952–56, CBS) | i. Neil Hamilton |
| 10. | "Private Secretary" (1953–57, CBS) | j. Ethel Waters |
| 11. | "Stanley" (1956–57, NBC) | k. Ann Sothern |
| 12. | "That Wonderful Guy" (1949–50, ABC) | l. Hume Cronyn |

Answers on page 221.

## MASTER QUIZ #1

I LOVE LUCY (1951–1961, CBS)

The title doesn't begin to explain the phenomenon that is this series. You see, everybody loved Lucy, and they always will. We can't remember a time when this series wasn't on television, whether first run or in syndication.

It remains unbelievably popular to this day, and the biggest reason why is Lucille Ball. Although surrounded by some excellent supporting characters, Lucy was the star unquestioned. Here are just a few questions to help you remember the many moments of joy that Lucy brought to us all.

1. What was Lucy's maiden name?

2. What club did Ricky perform at?

3. What was Lucy's seemingly constant desire?

4. Who played the Mertzes, the Ricardos' best friends as well as their neighbors and landlords?

5. Where did the series take place?

6. Where did the Ricardos move in 1957?

7. What did Ricky call his own nightclub?

8. Who played the role of Little Ricky?

9. What was the name of the medicine Lucy tried to do a commercial for?

10. According to one episode, what did George Washington say while crossing the Delaware?

11. Who are Harold Adamson and Eliot Daniel?

12. Who played the young boy who fell in love with Lucy after she gave him a dance lesson?

13. What instrument did Little Ricky play on the show?

14. How was Ricky dressed when his son was born?

15. What song did Ricky sing at the club when Lucy told him she was pregnant?

Answers on page 222.

## MASTER QUIZ #2

### THE HONEYMOONERS (1955–1956, CBS)

For the major percentage of its life on television, "The Honeymooners" appeared as a sketch within a show. Beginning first as a segment of Dumont's "Cavalcade of Stars" (1951) and then as part of "The Jackie Gleason Show" on CBS, "The Honeymooners" became a series of its own in 1955. Only 39 episodes were filmed, all in front of live audiences (a relatively new practice), and each one was a gem. Therefore we offer a master quiz of no small proportion on this all-time great series.

THE CAST:

| | |
|---|---|
| Ralph Kramden | Jackie Gleason |
| Ed Norton | Art Carney |
| Alice Kramden | Audrey Meadows |
| Trixie Norton | Joyce Randolph |

1. How did Norton describe his occupation as a sewer worker?

2. In an episode titled "The Baby-Sitter," in which the Kramdens had a phone, what was their phone number?

3. What was the name of the golf course where Ralph was to play with his boss, Mr. Marshall?

4. What was the name of the company Ralph worked for?

5. Who was the landlord of the Kramdens' building?

6. On what street was Norton hurt when a manhole cover hit him on the head?

7. What was the name of Norton's childhood pet dog?

8. Who portrayed the host of "The $99,000 Answer"?

9. What was the name of the dance teacher who moved into Ralph's building?

10. What was the name of Ralph's and Norton's bowling team, and who were they to play in the championship match?

11. Name the stars of the fictitious film, "Rhythm on Ice."

12. What two addresses were used as the Kramdens', one erroneously?

13. What magazine bought Ralph's story when he was supposedly dying of arterial monochromia?

14. What is Norton's diagnosis for the Kramdens' broken vacuum cleaner?

15. Where does Ralph go on his fishing trips?

16. Who was Uncle Leo's wife, and where did they live?

17. What magazine was Norton thrilled to find at the local barber shop?

18. Who left Ralph her "Fortune"?

19. Where is the Raccoon National Cemetery?

20. Which department store offers to redecorate the Kramdens' apartment?

21. Whose record for the all-time low gas bill does Ralph break?

22. Who does Norton replace in the play being staged by the Ladies Auxiliary of the Raccoons?

23. When Ralph and Norton take the wrong train to the Raccoon convention, where are they really headed?

24. With what company does Norton land a job when he is fired from the sewer?

25. What's Ralph's weekly salary? Norton's?

26. Where did Norton play handball?

27. When was Alice's birthday? Trixie's?

28. What was Ralph zodiacal sign? Ed's?

29. Where did the Kramdens and the Davises eat?

30. Who recorded "Claves for Mambo"?

31. Who was the Grand High Exalted Mystic Ruler?

32. Who was the "Donut King"?

33. Where did Norton supposedly study medicine?

34. What was Alice's sister's name? Who did she marry?

35. What planet did Norton say Captain Video was taking off for?

36. For whom did Norton buy a ring as a gift?

37. Where did Ralph win the horse with the clock in its stomach?

38. What was the room number at the IRS office when Ralph got called to report?

39. Who was the only officer of Ralph's company to appear on the show? (Hint: He appeared in the episode "The Golfer.")

40. What did Uncle Leo give Ralph and Alice for Christmas?

Answers on pages 222–223.

# Keep 'Em Laughing!

## THE ADDAMS FAMILY  (1964–1966, ABC)

1. What instrument did Lurch, the butler play?
2. What was Wednesday Addams's middle name?
3. Who played Grandmama? Cousin Itt?
4. What was Gomez Addams's trademark?

Answers on page 223.

## THE ANDY GRIFFITH SHOW  (1960–1968, CBS)

1. Who was Aunt Bea's (Frances Bavier's) best friend? Who played her?
2. What poem did Barney write for his sweetheart Juanita?
3. Who was Andy's first girl friend on the show? Who played her?
4. What was this series' syndicated title?

5. Who played the role of Floyd, the barber (1965–68)?

6. What type of business was Emmett Clark (1967–68) in?

Answers on page 223.

## BEWITCHED   (1964–1972, ABC)

1. We all know Endora (Agnes Moorehead) was Samantha's mother. Who was her father?

2. Where did Darrin work?

3. Who were the Stephens' neighbors? Who played them?

4. Who played Tabitha (1966–72)?

Answers on page 223.

## THE BILL COSBY SHOW   (1969–1971, NBC)

1. What character did Cosby play? His profession?

2. What two actresses played Bill's mother, Rose, on the show?

3. Who played co-worker Marsha Peterson?

Answers on page 224.

## THE BILL DANA SHOW   (1963–1965, NBC)

1. What character did Dana play?

2. Where did he work?

3. Who played the role of Byron Glick?

Answers on page 224.

## THE BING CROSBY SHOW   (1964–1965, ABC)

1. What character did Bing Crosby play?

2. What did he do for a living?
3. Who played Bing's wife, Ellie?

Answers on page 224.

## THE BRADY BUNCH (1969–1974, ABC)

1. Where did the Bradys live?
2. What was Mike Brady's profession?
3. There were six Brady kids. How many can you name?

Answers on page 224.

## CAPTAIN NICE (1967, ABC)

1. What was Captain Nice's real name? Who played him?
2. What did he do for a living?
3. Where did the Captain practice his crime-stopping?
4. Who played the Captain's wife?

Answers on page 224.

## CAR 54, WHERE ARE YOU? (1961–1963, NBC)

1. In what precinct did Toody and Muldoon work?
2. Who played the role of Lucille Toody, Gunther's wife?
3. Fred Gwynne would later star with a member of the cast of "Car 54" in another popular series. Who was he?
4. What was Toody's famous phrase?

Answers on page 224.

## THE COURTSHIP OF EDDIE'S FATHER
## (1969–1972, ABC)

1. Who played the role of housekeeper Mrs. Livingston?

2. What was Tom Corbett's profession? Who played him?

3. Who directed and starred in the series as Norman Tinker?

Answers on page 224.

## THE DEBBIE REYNOLDS SHOW   (1969–1970, NBC)

What was the occupation of Debbie's husband, Jim (Don Chastain)?

Answer on page 224.

## THE DORIS DAY SHOW   (1968–1973, CBS)

1. Where did Doris Martin work? Who was her boss?

2. Doris got a new boss at the start of the fourth season. Who was he?

3. What business did Doris live above when she moved to San Francisco?

Answers on page 225.

## F TROOP   (1965–1967, ABC)

1. What actors played Roaring Chicken, Bald Eagle, Flaming Arrow, and Wise Owl?

2. Who played the role of Wrangler Jane?

3. At what fort did the series take place?

4. With what Indian tribe did O'Rourke and Agarn have their business association? Who was their chief?

Answers on page 225.

## FAMILY AFFAIR   (1966–1971, CBS)

1. What was Bill Davis's occupation? Who played him?
2. What were his nephew's and nieces' names?
3. What was the name of the doll that was featured in the show?
4. Why did Mr. French supposedly leave the show? Who replaced him?

Answers on page 225.

## THE FARMER'S DAUGHTER   (1963–1966, ABC)

1. Who starred as "Katy" Holstrum?
2. What role did William Windom play?
3. How many sons did Windom's character have? Their names?
4. How did Agatha (Windom's mother) get up and down the stairs? Who played her?

Answers on page 225.

## THE FLYING NUN   (1967–1970, ABC)

1. What was Sister Bertrille's (Sally Field) name before she joined the convent?
2. At what convent was she living? Where was it?
3. Who played Sister Bertrille's Mother Superior?

Answers on page 225.

## GET SMART   (1965–1970, NBC and CBS)

1. Who was the head of K.A.O.S.? Who played him? Who was his aide?

2. What two well-known comedians created this series?

3. Who played Hymie, the robot?

4. Who was the agent who kept popping out of mailboxes, garbage cans, etc.?

Answers on page 225.

## THE GHOST AND MRS. MUIR (1968–1970, NBC and ABC)

1. Who was the ghost, and who played him?

2. Who was the ghost's nephew, and who played him?

3. Where was the series set?

Answers on page 226.

## GIDGET (1965–1966, ABC)

1. What was Gidget's real name?

2. Who was Gidget's best friend?

3. What did Gidget's father do for a living?

Answers on page 226.

## GILLIGAN'S ISLAND (1964–1967, CBS)

1. What was the name of the shipwrecked boat?

2. Who appeared on the show as a Hollywood producer? What show did the cast perform for him?

3. From what state was Maryann Summers (Dawn Wells)?

Answers on page 226.

## GOMER PYLE, U.S.M.C. (1964–1970, CBS)

1. Where was Gomer Pyle stationed?

2. Who was Sergeant Carter's (Frank Sutton) girl friend? Who played her?

3. What role did comedian Ronnie Schell play?

Answers on page 226.

## THE GOOD GUYS   (1968–1970, CBS)

1. Who were the two lead characters, and who played them?

2. What was the name of the diner used as the setting?

3. Who played the role of regular customer Big Tom?

Answers on page 226.

## GOOD MORNING, WORLD   (1967–1968, CBS)

1. Who owned the radio station that Dave Lewis and Larry Clarke worked at?

2. Who played Lewis's neighbor Sandy?

Answers on page 226.

## THE GOVERNOR AND J.J.   (1969–1972, CBS)

1. What did "J.J." stand for? Who played her?

2. What type of dog did J.J. take in? What was his name?

3. What role did dancer-actor Dan Dailey play?

Answers on page 226.

## GREEN ACRES   (1965–1971, CBS)

1. Who owned the general store?

2. Who were the carpenters the Douglases hired to rebuild their house?

3. Who owned the pig that played such a prominent role in the series?

Answers on page 227.

## HAZEL   (1961–1966, NBC, CBS)

1. During this series's run, Hazel worked for two families. Who were they?

2. What was George Baxter's profession? Who played him?

3. Who played George's wife and son, Dorothy and Harold?

Answers on page 227.

## HE & SHE   (1967–1970, CBS)

1. Who played Dick Hollister? What cartoon character did he create?

2. Who played that same cartoon character when it was made into a television program?

3. What was Paula Hollister's occupation? Who played her?

Answers on page 227.

## HEY LANDLORD   (1966–1967, NBC)

1. Who was the landlord?

2. How did he come to own the building?

3. Who did the landlord share his own apartment with?

Answers on page 227.

## HOGAN'S HEROES   (1965–1971, CBS)

1. At what POW camp did this series take place?
2. Ivan Dixon played Corporal Kinchloe from 1965 to 1969. Who replaced him in that role in 1969?
3. What were Colonel Klink's secretaries' names? (There were two.)

Answers on page 227.

## I DREAM OF JEANNIE   (1965–1970, NBC)

1. How old was Jeannie?
2. Where did Tony Nelson live?
3. Did Tony ever marry Jeannie?

Answers on page 227.

## I'M DICKENS—HE'S FENSTER   (1962–1963, ABC)

Who played Arch Fenster and Harry Dickens? What was their profession?

Answer on page 227.

## IT'S ABOUT TIME   (1966–1967, CBS)

1. What were the two astronauts' names who broke the time barrier?
2. The astronauts made friends with a cave family played by Imogene Coca, Joe E. Ross, Mary Grace, and Pat Cardi. What were their cave names?

Answers on page 228.

## THE JOEY BISHOP SHOW   (1961–1965, NBC and CBS)

1. What role did Joey Bishop play? What was his profession?
2. Joey had two wives during this series run. Who were they?

Answers on page 228.

## JULIA   (1968–1971, NBC)

1. What company did Julia (Diahann Carrol) work for?
2. Who played Julia's son, Corey?
3. Who were Julia's neighbors? What did the husband do?

Answers on page 228.

## THE LUCY SHOW   (1962–1974, CBS)

1. During this series's run, Lucy lived in three cities. What were they?
2. Where did Lucy work in each of the cities?
3. What title-change did the series undergo in 1968?

Answers on page 228.

## MAYBERRY, R.F.D.   (1968–1971, CBS)

1. Who played the role of farmer Sam Jones?
2. Who was Sam's girl friend? Who played her?
3. In 1970, Aunt Bee was replaced by Aunt Alice. Who played her?

Answers on page 228.

## McHALE'S NAVY   (1962–1966, ABC)

1. What nickname did McHale's group have for Captain Binghampton (Joe Flynn)?

2. To what Italian city was the entire cast relocated in the show's last season?

Answers on page 228.

## MICKEY   (1964–1965, ABC)

1. Where was the hotel that Mickey inherited? What was it called?

2. What bank held the mortgage on the hotel?

3. Who played Mickey's son, Timmy Grady?

Answers on page 228.

## MR. TERRIFIC   (1967, CBS)

1. What was Mr. Terrific's real name, and who played him? What was his occupation?

2. What government agency developed the secret pills used to become Mr. Terrific? Who was the agency head?

3. Why did the government choose this particular ordinary fellow to become a super crime fighter?

Answers on page 229.

## THE MONKEES   (1966–1968, NBC)

Name the members of the Monkees.

Answer on page 229.

## THE MOTHERS-IN-LAW  (1967–1969, NBC)

1. What two actors played the role of Roger Buell?
2. What was Roger Buell's occupation? Herb Hubbard's?
3. What connection did Eve Hubbard (Eve Arden) have with the sporting world?

Answers on page 229.

## THE MUNSTERS  (1964–1966, CBS)

1. What was the Munsters' address?
2. Where did Herman work?
3. What kind of doll did Eddie Munster have?
4. How old was Herman Munster?

Answers on page 229.

## MY FAVORITE MARTIAN  (1963–1966, CBS)

1. Who played Uncle Martin and Tim O'Hara?
2. What paper did Tim work for?
3. Who was their next-door neighbor? Who played her?

Answers on page 229.

## MY LIVING DOLL  (1964–1965, CBS)

1. What was different about Rhoda Miller (Julie Newmar)?
2. What was Bob Cummings' name and profession on the show?

Answers on page 229.

## MY MOTHER THE CAR   (1965–1966, NBC)

1. Who was the voice of the car? What make was it?
2. Who played antique car collector and bad guy Captain Mancini?
3. What were Dave Crabtree's kids' names?

Answers on page 229.

## MY THREE SONS   (1960–1972, ABC and CBS)

1. Who played Steve Douglas' father-in-law, "Bub" O'Casey (1960–64)?
2. Who played son Mike (1960–65)? Why did Mike leave home?
3. To where did the Douglas family move in 1967?
4. What did Robbie and Katie name their triplets? Who played the triplets (1970–72)?

Answers on page 230.

## MY WORLD AND WELCOME TO IT   (1969–1972, NBC and CBS)

1. What was John Monroe's occupation? Who played him?
2. Who played his wife, Ellen, and daughter, Lydia?
3. On whose work was this series based?

Answers on page 230.

## NO TIME FOR SERGEANTS   (1964–1965, ABC)

1. Who played Airman Will Stockdale?
2. At what base was he stationed?

Answers on page 230.

# THE PATTY DUKE SHOW   (1963–1966, ABC)

1. What was Patty's brother's name? Who played him?
2. Where did the Lanes live?
3. Who was Patty's boyfriend? What job did he hold?

Answers on page 230.

# PETTICOAT JUNCTION   (1963–1970, CBS)

1. During the series's run, there were three Billie Jo Bradleys, two Bobbie Jo Bradleys and one Betty Jo Bradley. How many can you name?
2. In what city was the Shady Rest Hotel?
3. Who played Kate Bradley (1963–69) and Uncle Joe Carson?

Answers on page 230.

# PLEASE DON'T EAT THE DAISIES   (1965–1967, NBC)

1. Where did Jim Nash teach English?
2. Who were the Nashes' next-door neighbors?
3. What was Joan Nash's occupation?

Answers on page 230.

# THE SECOND HUNDRED YEARS   (1967–1968, ABC)

1. How did Luke Carpenter die? Who played him?
2. Who played Luke's father, Edwin Carpenter?
3. Where did Edwin Carpenter live?

Answers on page 230.

## TAMMY   (1965–1966, ABC)

1. What was Tammy's last name, and who played her?
2. Who played Tammy's grandpa?
3. For whom did Tammy work as a secretary?

Answers on page 231.

## THAT GIRL   (1966–1971, ABC)

1. Who was "That Girl"?
2. Who was her boyfriend? Who played him? Where did he work?
3. Were they ever married on the show?
4. Where did "That Girl's" parents live?

Answers on page 231.

## TO ROME WITH LOVE   (1969–1971, CBS)

1. Who played Michael Endicott, and what was his occupation?
2. From where did Endicott move, and why?
3. What were Endicott's daughters' names?

Answers on page 231.

Below you will find a list of fifteen popular situation comedies from the 1960s. Can you match the show with its star?

1. "Baileys of Balboa" (1964–65, CBS)    a. Dick Kallman
2. "Camp Runamuck" (1965–66, NBC)    b. Peter Duel

3. "Double Life of Henry     c. Peter Kastner
   Phyfe" (1966, ABC)
4. "Ensign O'Toole"        d. Red Buttons
   (1962–64, NBC and ABC)
5. "Hank" (1965–66, NBC)   e. Burl Ives
6. "The Hathaways"       f. Peggy Cass
   (1961–62, ABC)
7. "Love on a Rooftop"    g. Paul Ford
   (1966–71, ABC)
8. "Mr. Deeds Goes to      h. Monte Markham
   Town" (1969–70, ABC)
9. "Mona McCluskey"      i. Dean Jones
   (1965–66, NBC)
10. "O.K. Crackerby" (1965–66, ABC)  j. Tim Conway
11. "Occasional Wife"     k. Dave Ketchum
   (1966–67, NBC)
12. "Pete and Gladys"     l. Tony Franciosa
   (1960–62, CBS)
13. "Rango" (1967, ABC)    m. Michael Callan
14. "Ugliest Girl in Town"   n. Harry Morgan
   (1968–69, ABC)
15. "Valentine's Day"      o. Juliet Prowse
   (1964–65, ABC)

Answers on page 231.

## MASTER QUIZ #1

### THE BEVERLY HILLBILLIES (1962–1971, CBS)

This was one of the most popular situation comedies ever produced, as indicated by its long stay on TV screens throughout America. People thrilled to the idea of a poor family striking it rich, and they tuned in regularly to live through each new adventure encountered by the "rags-to-riches" Clampett family. Here's a quiz based on the show.

1. What was Granny's real name? Who played her?

2. Who played Milburn Drysdale, Margaret Drysdale, and their son Sonny Drysdale?

3. Who sang the show's theme?

4. What fictitious Hollywood star did Elly Mae fall for?

5. How did Elly May describe her new built-in swimming pool?

6. Where did the Clampetts live before moving to Beverly Hills?

7. At what bank did Milburn Drysdale work? Who was his secretary?

8. What was the name of Mrs. Drysdale's prized poodle?

9. Who played cousin Pearl Bodine?

10. What movie studio did the Clampetts purchase?

Answers on page 231.

## MASTER QUIZ #2

THE DICK VAN DYKE SHOW   (1961–1966, CBS)

This series can best be described as a "natural" sitcom. Viewers felt right at home with the Petries. They were a basic family unit living life in the suburbs, encountering everyday problems, and tackling each one comically. The cast was exceptional in every way. Here's a quiz on one of our personal favorites.

1. Who did Rob Petrie write comedy for?

2. Who were his co-writers? Who played them?

3. What was Richie Petrie's middle name?

4. What was the occupation of Rob's neighbor Jerry?

5. What character did Richard Deacon play?

6. Where did the Petries live?

7. What type of animal was Richie's pet "Stanley"?

8. What did you get when you connected the freckles on Rob's back?

9. What had been Laura's previous career?

10. When Laura had Richie, Rob was convinced that the hospital had made an error and given them the wrong baby. What was the name of the couple who Rob thought had his real baby?

Answers on page 232.

# THEY'RE STILL LAUGHING!

## ALL IN THE FAMILY   (1971–1980, CBS)

1. What was the Bunkers' address?
2. Where did Archie work? He moonlighted doing what?
3. What series were "spun off" from "All in the Family"?
4. What was Edith's maiden name?

Answers on page 232.

## ALL'S FAIR   (1976–1977, CBS)

1. Who played Richard Barrington and Charlotte Drake?
2. What did these two characters do for a living?
3. What city served as a setting for this series?

Answers on page 232.

## ARNIE   (1970–1972), CBS

1. What was Arnie's last name, and who played him?

2. Who played Lillian, his wife?

3. Who was Arnie's boss? What was the company's name?

Answers on page 232.

## THE BAD NEWS BEARS   (1979–1980, CBS)

1. What school team did Morris Buttermaker coach? Who played him?

2. What job did Buttermaker hold before becoming a coach?

3. What was Buttermaker's female pitcher's name?

Answers on page 232.

## BALL FOUR   (1976, CBS)

1. What baseball team did this series chronicle?

2. Who was the team's manager, and who played him?

3. What character did Jim Bouton play?

Answers on page 233.

## BAREFOOT IN THE PARK   (1970–1971, ABC)

1. In what city did this series take place?

2. Who played the newly wed Bratters (Paul and Corie)?

Answers on page 233.

## BARNEY MILLER   (1975–1981, ABC)

1. Where was the 12th Precinct?

2. What were Barney's kids' names?

3. What was the title of Detective Harris' book about the stationhouse escapades?

Answers on page 233.

## BLANSKY'S BEAUTIES   (1977, ABC)

1. Who played the lead role of Nancy Blansky?
2. Nancy staged shows at what Las Vegas hotel?
3. Who played showgirl Bambi Benton?

Answers on page 233.

## BOB & CAROL & TED & ALICE   (1973, ABC)

1. How many of the four leading character actors can you name?
2. What did Bob Sanders do for a living? Ted Henderson?

Answers on page 233.

## THE BOB CRANE SHOW   (1975, NBC)

1. What did Bob Wilcox do for a living?
2. Why did Bob quit his job?
3. Who was Bob's landlord? Who played him?

Answers on page 233.

## THE BOB NEWHART SHOW   (1972–1978, CBS)

1. In what city did this series take place?
2. What veteran of another popular sitcom played Mrs. Bakerman, one of Bob's patients?
3. Who was Howard Borden's brother, and what was his profession?

Answers on page 233.

## THE BRIAN KEITH SHOW   (1972–1974, NBC)

1. What role did Brian Keith play?
2. Who played his daughter on the series?
3. Where did the series take place?

Answers on page 233.

## BRIDGET LOVES BERNIE   (1972–1973, CBS)

1. Who played the title roles?
2. What was Bridget's occupation?
3. Bernie was a writer, but he made ends meet by doing something else too. What was his second career?

Answers on page 234.

## C.P.O. SHARKEY   (1976–1978, NBC)

1. Where was C.P.O. Sharkey stationed?
2. Who was the base commander?

Answers on page 234.

## CALUCCI'S DEPARTMENT   (1973, CBS)

1. Who played Joe Calucci?
2. Where did Joe work?
3. Joe fell in love with his secretary, played by Candy Azzara. What was her character's name?

Answers on page 234.

## CARTER COUNTRY   (1977–1979, ABC)

1. What town was the setting for this series?

2. Who was Carter?

3. Who played Chief Roy Mobey?

Answers on page 234.

## THE CHICAGO TEDDY BEARS   (1971, CBS)

1. What type of business did Linc McCray and his Uncle Latzi own?

2. Who played these two characters?

3. Nick Marr was played by what comedian-turned-actor?

Answers on page 234.

## CHICO AND THE MAN   (1974–1978, NBC)

1. Who wrote the theme song for this series?

2. What was Ed's ("The Man's") last name? Who played him?

3. Who played Chico's aunt (1977–78)?

Answers on page 234.

## THE CORNER BAR   (1972–1973, ABC)

1. What was the name of the bar on "The Corner Bar"?

2. Who played Harry Grant, the owner?

3. Shimen Ruskin played a waiter. What was the character's name?

4. What was Fred Costello's occupation? Donald Hooten's?

Answers on page 234.

## DIANA   (1973–1974, NBC)

1. Where did Diana (Diana Rigg) work?
2. Who was her neighbor?

Answers on page 235.

## DOC   (1975–1976, CBS)

1. Who played "Doc" Joe Bogert?
2. In what city was this series located?
3. Who ran the Westside Clinic, where "Doc" worked? Who played this character?

Answers on page 235.

## THE DON RICKLES SHOW   (1972, CBS)

1. Where did Don Robinson work?
2. Where did the Robinsons live?
3. What actress played Barbara Robinson, Don's wife?

Answers on page 235.

## FUNNY FACE   (1971, CBS)

1. What actress-dancer-singer played the lead role in this series?
2. Where did the lead character attend college?

Answers on page 235.

## THE GOOD LIFE   (1971–1972, NBC)

1. What two stars (currently two of the hottest "properties" on television) starred in the roles of Albert and Jane Miller?

2. What did they do for a living?

3. Who was their boss?

Answers on page 235.

## GRANDPA GOES TO WASHINGTON
(1978–1979, NBC)

1. How did Senator Joe Kelley get elected? Who played him?

2. Who played his son? What was the character's name?

3. What type of car did Joe Kelley drive?

Answers on page 235.

## HAPPY DAYS   (1974–1983, ABC)

1. What high school did Richie Cunningham attend? In what city was the school?

2. The first "Happy Days" episode appeared as a segment of what show?

3. Who were the two owners of Arnold's Drive-In?

4. When Richie and Ralph joined the army, where were they stationed?

Answers on page 235.

## HOT L BALTIMORE   (1975, ABC)

1. What was Hot L Baltimore?

2. Who played desk clerk Bill Lewis?

3. Who was the hotel manager?

Answers on page 236.

# THE JIMMY STEWART SHOW   (1971–1972, NBC)

1. At what school did Professor James K. Howard teach?
2. What subject did he teach?
3. Where did the Howards live?

*Answers on page 236.*

# LOTSA LUCK   (1973–1974, NBC)

1. What character did Dom DeLuise portray?
2. Who played Stanley's wife?
3. What were Stanley's sister's and brother-in-law's names?

*Answers on page 236.*

# M*A*S*H   (1972–1983, CBS)

1. What does M*A*S*H stand for?
2. Where was the plane carrying Colonel Henry Blake shot down?
3. Who did Major Houlihan marry?
4. Where was Corporal "Radar" O'Reilly born?

*Answers on page 236.*

# MAUDE   (1972–1978, CBS)

1. Where did Maude and her family live?
2. What business did Walter Findlay own?
3. Who played the Findlays neighbors?

*Answers on page 236.*

## THE McCLEAN STEVENSON SHOW
(1976–1977, NBC)

1. Where did Mac Ferguson live?
2. What type of business did he own?
3. Who played Mac's ex-wife, Peggy?

Answers on page 236.

## MORK & MINDY   (1978–1981, ABC)

1. Where did Mork land?
2. Who was his Orkan leader?
3. Who played Mindy's dad, and what type of business did he run?

Answers on page 236.

## THE NANCY WALKER SHOW   (1976, ABC)

1. What character did Nancy play?
2. What was her profession?
3. Where did she live?
4. How often did she see her husband? Who played him?

Answers on page 237.

## NANNY AND THE PROFESSOR   (1970–1971, ABC)

1. Whom did Phoebe Figalilly replace as Nanny?
2. Who played Professor Howard Everett?
3. What were the Everett children's names?

Answers on page 237.

## THE NEW ANDY GRIFFITH SHOW   (1971, CBS)

1. What role did Andy Griffith play in this series?
2. Why did he return home to Greenwood, leaving a government job at the state capital?
3. Who played Lee, Andy's wife?

Answers on page 237.

## THE NEW DICK VAN DYKE SHOW
(1971–1974, CBS)

1. Where did the Prestons live?
2. Who played Jenny Preston, Dick's wife?
3. Where did the Prestons move to, and why?

Answers on page 237.

## ON THE ROCKS   (1975–1976, ABC)

1. What prison served as a setting for this series?
2. Who played inmates Fuentes and Cleaver?

Answers on page 237.

## OPERATION PETTICOAT   (1977–1979, ABC)

1. Who played Lieutenant Commander Matthew Sherman?
2. What was the name of the submarine he commanded? What color was it?

Answers on page 237.

## PAPER MOON   (1974–1975, ABC)

1. What state served as a setting for this show?

2. Who played the roles of Moses Pray and Addie Pray?

Answers on page 237.

## THE PARTRIDGE FAMILY (1970–1974, ABC)

1. What did the Partridge family use for transportation?
2. Who was the band's agent? Who played him?
3. How many of the five Partridge kids can you name?

Answers on page 238.

## THE PAUL LYNDE SHOW (1972–1973, ABC)

1. Where did Paul Simms and his family live?
2. What was odd about Paul's son-in-law Howie?
3. Who played Barney and Grace Dickerson, Howie's parents?

Answers on page 238.

## PAUL SAND IN FRIENDS AND LOVERS (1974–1975, CBS)

1. What was Robert Dreyfuss' profession?
2. Who played Robert's dad, Ben?
3. Fred Mayerbach was one of Robert's co-workers. Who played him?

Answers on page 238.

## PHYLLIS (1975–1977, CBS)

1. Where did Phyllis move after the death of her husband, Lars?
2. Where did Phyllis work?

3. Who played Phyllis' mother-in-law's husband's mother?

Answers on page 238.

## POPI  (1976, CBS)

1. On what movie was this series based?
2. Who played the role of "Popi" (Abraham Rodriquez), and where did he live?
3. What were Rodriquez's two sons named?

Answers on page 238.

## RHODA  (1974–1978, CBS)

1. Who did Rhoda marry? What company did he own?
2. Where did Rhoda work in the later episodes?
3. Who played Brenda Morganstern, Rhoda's sister? Her boyfriend?

Answers on page 238.

## SANFORD AND SON  (1972–1977, CBS)

1. What was Aunt Esther's husband's name?
2. Who played Fred's girl friend Donna Harris?
3. Whitman Mayo and Don Bexley played two of Fred's friends. Which two?

Answers on page 238.

## STOCKARD CHANNING IN JUST FRIENDS  (1979, CBS)

1. At what health spa did Susan Hughes work?

2. Susan Hughes moved from one city to another. Name the two cities.

Answers on page 239.

## TABITHA   (1977–1978, ABC)

1. Who played the title role of Tabitha Stevens?
2. Where did Tabitha work?
3. Who played Tabitha's Aunt Minerva?

Answers on page 239.

## TEMPERATURES RISING   (1972–1974, ABC)

1. What hospital was the setting for this series?
2. Who played Drs. Noland and Mercy?

Answers on page 239.

## THE TONY RANDALL SHOW
## (1976–1978, ABC and CBS)

1. What character did Tony Randall play?
2. Daughter Roberta was played by two actresses during this series' run. Can you name both?
3. Who played Randall's father on the show?

Answers on page 239.

## THE WAVERLY WONDERS   (1978, NBC)

1. Aside from coaching basketball at Waverly High, what other job did Joe Casey hold at the school?
2. Who played Joe Casey?
3. Where was Waverly High?

Answers on page 239.

## WELCOME BACK KOTTER (1975–1979, ABC)

1. What school served as a setting for this series?
2. What did the Kotters name their twins?
3. What character did John Sylvester White play?

Answers on page 239.

## WHEN THINGS WERE ROTTEN (1975, ABC)

1. Who played Robin Hood in this spoof?
2. Who played Friar Tuck and Alan-a-Dale?
3. Who created this series?

Answers on page 239.

We feel that we've been much too easy on you folks, so we're throwing in a twist this time. We're only listing members of the fairer sex this time to make it a bit tougher. Good luck! You'll need it this time! No more Mr. Nice Guy!

| | | | |
|---|---|---|---|
| 1. | "Adam's Rib" (1973, ABC) | a. | Sheree North |
| 2. | "Angie" (1979–80, ABC) | b. | Geraldine Brooks |
| 3. | "Anna and the King" (1972, CBS) | c. | Florence Stanley |
| 4. | "Big Eddie" (1975, CBS) | d. | Donna Pescow |
| 5. | "Busting Loose" (1977, ABC) | e. | Tricia & Cyb Barnstable |
| 6. | "The Dumplings" (1976, NBC) | f. | Deirdre Lenihan |
| 7. | "Dusty's Trail" (1973; syndicated) | g. | Barbara Rhodes |
| 8. | "Holmes and Yo Yo" (1976, ABC) | h. | Bess Armstrong |
| 9. | "Joe and Sons" (1975–76, CBS) | i. | Blythe Danner |

| | |
|---|---|
| 10. "Me and the Chimp" (1972, CBS) | j. Dena Dietrich |
| 11. "Needles and Pins" (1973, NBC) | k. Andrea Howard |
| 12. "On Our Own" (1977–78, CBS) | l. Samantha Eggar |
| 13. "The Practice" (1976–77, NBC) | m. Anita Gillette |
| 14. "Quark" (1978, NBC) | n. Jeannine Riley |
| 15. "The Super" (1972, ABC) | o. Ardell Sheridan |

Answers on pages 240–241.

## MASTER QUIZ # 1

### THE MARY TYLER MOORE SHOW
(1970–1977, CBS)

Years after her role as Laura Petrie on "The Dick Van Dyke Show" established her as one of the television audience's favorite ladies, Mary Tyler Moore returned to star in this long-running and tremendously popular series. The cast represented a great cross-section of people with whom we all come into contact, from pompous Ted Baxter to gruff but fatherly Lou Grant, all portrayed beautifully by this superb group. Here is a quiz on this popular TV sitcom.

1. What city was the series set in?

2. At what television station did Mary Richards work? Who played her boss?

3. Who was the head writer for the news? Who played him?

4. What was Georgette Baxter's maiden name?

5. What was the name of Ted and Georgette's adopted son?

6. What was the name of Sue Ann Niven's TV program?

7. What was Lou Grant's wife's first name? Who played her?

8. What was the name of the theme song for "The Mary Tyler Moore Show"?

9. How did Ted Baxter always begin telling his life story?

10. Who played Gordie, the member of the news team who eventually made it big on another network? What did Ted call Gordie?

Answers on page 240.

## MASTER QUIZ # 2

### THE ODD COUPLE   (1970–1975, ABC)

Most people generally agree that "The Odd Couple" is one of the finest series ever produced on television. It is usually mentioned in the same breath with "The Honeymooners," "All in the Family," "M*A*S*H," and "The Phil Silvers Show," and rightly so. The key word here was consistency. Each show provided us with some priceless bits of nonsense that stayed with us long after the final credits.

In addition, "The Odd Couple" has probably introduced more phrases from its scripts into our everyday language than any other series. How many times have you used these phrases?

*"Il forza del destino!"*
"Now I know your true colors."
"Who are you, Jacques Cousteau?"
"Oscar, Oscar, Oscar!"

These examples don't even begin to scratch the surface. The series is as popular today as it ever was, running in syndication all over the country, sometimes more than once a day! In tribute to this great, great series, we offer the following master quiz. Show us your true colors.

1. Who was Oscar's bookie?

2. Who was Felix's doctor? What doctor performed surgery on Oscar?

3. To what island did the boys go for a vacation?

4. Where did Felix and Gloria go on their honeymoon?

5. Felix was arrested for supposedly scalping tickets to what play?

6. What was the name of the racing dog Oscar won in a card game? Who did he win it from? Where did the boys race him?

7. What was the corporate name of Felix's business?

8. What fat farm did the boys go to?

9. What was Felix's parrot's name?

10. A blind man (Scatman Crothers) gave Felix a puppy from his dog's litter, which Felix helped deliver aboard a train. What did Felix name the dog?

11. As what did the boys dress when they appeared on "Let's Make a Deal"?

12. What did Ocar's mother do when she got nervous or upset?

13. What two opera singers appeared on the show?

14. Which burial plot did Felix want to buy?

15. Who played the owner of *Harum* magazine?

16. Who originally played Edna Unger, Felix's daughter?

17. What was the name of the guard dog at the security apartment the boys moved into?

18. Oscar attempted to do some ad photos for what cologne?

19. Felix coached his son's football team for one game. What football play did Felix suggest to the team?

20. What did Felix title his poem about a new high rise?

Answers on page 240.

# TELEVISION'S BEST FRIEND

A NIMALS HOLD A WARM SPOT IN ALL OUR hearts, and it's been no different on television. We are always amazed at how a pet can become such an integral part of the family unit, and nowhere was this more apparent than television, with series like "Flipper" and "Lassie."

Millions tuned in with loyal regularity to thrill as Lassie saved yet another helpless human being, risking her own life to save that of someone in trouble.

On the following pages you will find a few questions on some of the most popular animal series ever produced for television. Also, you will be tested on how well you can remember some famous (and some not so famous) televison house pets.

## THE ADVENTURES OF CHAMPION
(1955–1956, CBS)

1. Who owned Champion, the Wonder Horse? Who played him?

2. Who owned the ranch the horse stayed on?

3. How many people did Champion allow to ride him?

Answers on page 241.

## THE ADVENTURES OF RIN TIN TIN
(1954–1959, ABC)

1. Who owned the brave dog, Rin Tin Tin?

2. The soldiers at what fort "adopted" the boy and his dog?

3. Who was Rin Tin Tin's trainer?

Answers on page 241.

## FLIPPER   (1964–1968, NBC)

1. Who played the role of Flipper?

2. Who played Porter Ricks? He was chief ranger of what park?

3. How many children did Porter have and what were their names?

Answers on page 241.

## GENTLE BEN   (1967–1969, CBS)

1. Who played the role of Tom Wedloe on the series?

2. His son, Mark, was played by what child actor?

3. What type of bear was Ben?

4. Where did the Wedloes live?

Answers on page 241.

## LASSIE   (1954–1971, CBS)

1. Lassie had many owners during her long stay on television sets across America. Who was her first owner? Who played him?

2. In what town was Lassie originally located?

3. Lassie's second owner was played by Tom Provost. Whom did he portray?

4. Ruth Martin, who along with her husband bought the Miller farm, was played by two actresses from 1957 to 1964. Who were they?

Answers on page 241.

## MR. ED   (1961–1965, CBS)

1. Who played Mr. Ed's owner, Wilbur Post?

2. Who was the voice of Mr. Ed?

3. What did Wilbur do for a living?

Answers on page 241.

## MY FRIEND FLICKA   (1956–1958, CBS and NBC)

1. What type of animal was Flicka?

2. Who owned Flicka? Who played him?

3. In what state was the series located?

Answers on page 242.

## FIND MY OWNER

Here's a list of pets that played prominent roles in some popular television series. Can you name the type of pet and the series in which it was featured? Good luck!

1. Muffit
2. Stormy and Bandie
3. Silver and Scout
4. Buttons
5. Spot and Igor
6. Kitty
7. Tramp
8. Waldo and Myrtle
9. Ladadog
10. Oregano
11. Neil
12. Tornado and Phantom
13. Bingo
14. Jasper
15. Fred
16. Max
17. Tiger
18. Arnold
19. Bimbo
20. Clarence and Judy
21. Scruffy
22. Charlie, Enoch and Cindy
23. Gin-Gin
24. King
25. Chipper
26. Simone
27. Muffin
28. Trigger, Buttermilk, and Bullet
29. Yukon King and Rex
30. Cheetah
31. Cleo
32. Bruce
33. Snow
34. Nelson
35. Ginger and LuLu

Answers on page 243.

# TELEVISION GRAB BAG

**T**HIS SECTION OF THE BOOK IS OUR STORM drain, if you will. You know how it works; the rain comes down, creating a stream, which picks up debris on its way to the storm drain, but when the rain stops, the water disappears but the debris is left.

Well, this is our debris! Within the next few pages you will find tough quizzes based on nothing in particular. We just knew you would be in the mood for some tough questions after breezing through the rest of this book, so this is where we collected them for you, just as our storm drain collected the debris.

This section is guaranteed to bring back a lot of memories you didn't even know were locked inside your mind. We guarantee that at least once, you'll catch yourself saying, "Oh, yeah! I remember that show!"

So full-steam ahead into our catchall section, and if you make it through this one without really embarrassing yourself, you just might be ready for what's next!

What's in a name? A show is a show is a show! Can you match these original series titles with their alternate or rerun titles? There are many clues, so read carefully.

| 1. "Assignment Vienna" | a. "Badge 714" |
| 2. "Big Town" | b. "The Brian Keith Show" |
| 3. "Death Valley Days" | c. "City Assignment" |
| 4. "Doorway to Danger" | d. "Oh, Susanna" |
| 5. "Dragnet" | e. "The Men From Shiloh" |
| 6. "Foreign Intrigue" | f. "Martin Kane, Private Eye" |
| 7. "The Gale Storm Show" | g. "Cross Current" |
| 8. "Harbourmaster" | h. "Call of the West" |
| 9. "The Little People" | i. "Adventures at Scott Island" |
| 10. "Target—The Corrupters" | j. "Major Adams, Trailmaster" |
| 11. "The Virginian" | k. "Door With No Name" |
| 12. "Wagon Train" | l. "Expose" |

Answers on page 243.

Below is a list of TV's crime drama series. Can you match the series with its star?

| 1. "Adventures of Fu Manchu" (1955–56; syndicated) | a. Ben Gazzara |
| 2. "Amazing Mr. Malone" (1951–52, ABC) | b. Robert Carroll |
| 3. "Arrest and Trial" (1963–64, ABC) | c. Broderick Crawford |
| 4. "Barney Blake, Police Reporter" (1948, NBC) | d. Gary Merrill |
| 5. "The Court of Last Resort" (1957–60, NBC and ABC) | e. Glen Gordon |
| 6. "The Gallery of Mme. Leu-Tsong" (1951, Dumont) | f. Lyle Bettger |
| 7. "King of Diamonds" (1961–62; syndicated) | g. Marvin Miller |
| 8. "The Mask" (1954, ABC) | h. Lee Tracy |
| 9. "Mysteries of Chinatown" (1949–50, ABC) | i. Chuck Webster |

| | | | |
|---|---|---|---|
| 10. | "Photocrime" (1949, ABC) | j. | Anna May Wong |
| 11. | "The Stranger" (1954–55, Dumont) | k. | Walter Greaza |
| 12. | "Treasury Men in Action" (1950–55, ABC and NBC) | l. | Gene O'Donnell |

Answers on page 243.

Spinoffs are an invention of TV created to take advantage of a popular series, hoping that the TV audience will also respond favorably to a new show featuring characters from an already popular series. Can you match the spinoff on the right with its "papa" series on the left?

| | | | |
|---|---|---|---|
| 1. | "Ironside" | a. | "The Prisoner" |
| 2. | "Happy Days" | b. | "Surfside Six" |
| 3. | "Rockford Files" | c. | "Peter and Gladys" |
| 4. | "Trackdown" | d. | "The Jeffersons" |
| 5. | "Burke's Law" | e. | "The Sandy Duncan Show" |
| 6. | "Secret Agent" | f. | "Good Times" |
| 7. | "Empire" | g. | "Honey West" |
| 8. | "Maude" | h. | "Out of the Blue" |
| 9. | "December Bride" | i. | "Wanted: Dead or Alive" |
| 10. | "Funny Face" | j. | "Richie Brockelman, Private Eye" |
| 11. | "All in the Family" | k. | "Sarge" |
| 12. | "Bourbon Street Beat" | l. | "Redigo" |

Answers on page 243.

## YOUR HOST FOR THE EVENING

The following list is made up of TV shows that had a host to guide you through each week's activities. Do you know who hosted the following anthology series?

1. "Alcoa Premiere" (1961–63, ABC)

2. "Alcoa Presents" (1959–61, ABC)

3. "Cowboy Theater" (1957, NBC)

4. "Damon Runyon Theater" (1955–56, CBS)

5. "Favorite Story" (1952–54; syndicate)

6. "Frontier Justice" (1958–61, CBS) There were three hosts. Can you name all of them?

7. "General Electric Theater" (1953–62, CBS)

8. "Ghost Story" (1972–73, NBC)

9. "Omnibus" (1953–57, CBS and ABC)

10. "Schlitz Playhouse of Stars" (1951–59, CBS). Who was the host during the 1952 season?

11. "Silver Theater" (1949–50, CBS)

12. "Suspicion" (1957–59, NBC). Who was the original host of this series?

13. "20th Century Fox Hour" (1955–57, CBS). Can you name both hosts of this series?

14. "Warner Brothers Presents" (1955–56, ABC)

15. "West Point Story" (1956–58, CBS and ABC)

Answers on pages 243–244.

## NAME THAT TV THEME!

Below we supply you with a list of popular TV series. What we'd like you to try and do is name the theme song for each of the shows. This one should drive you crazy! You get half credit for being able to hum the song, but you're an expert only if you come up with the title. Good luck!

1. "Alfred Hitchcock Presents" (1955–56, CBS and NBC)

2. "The Courtship of Eddie's Father" (1969–72), ABC)

3. "Dr. Kildare" (1961–66, NBC)

4. "The Donna Reed Show" (1958–66, ABC)

5. "Dragnet" (1952–70, NBC)

6. "The Gene Autry Show" (1950–56, CBS)

7. "The Burns & Allen Show" (1950–58, CBS)

8. "The Greatest Show on Earth" (1963–64, ABC)

9. "Gunsmoke" (1957–73, CBS)

10. "The Lone Ranger" (1949–57, ABC)

11. "M*A*S*H" (1972–83, CBS)

12. "Medic" (1954–56, NBC)

13. "The Paper Chase" (1974–75, ABC)

14. "The Partridge Family" (1970–74, ABC)

15. "The Roy Rogers Show" (1951–57, NBC)

Answers on page 244.

# TOTAL TV OBSCURITY!

**W**ELL, YOU ARE A RARE INDIVIDUAL INDEED IF you've made it this far through our book without coming down with an acute case of "TV Trivia Wackos." But, merciless as we are, we are not about to let you catch your breath. This chapter contains questions that should only be undertaken by the strong-of-heart trivia buff. Many of these questions can only be answered by a true trivia expert, so don't get too frustrated.

Read on, you brave souls, and begin your journey with an obscure potpourri of really tough ones. Good luck!

1. What role did Alan Young play on "The Alan Young Show" (1950–53; CBS)?

2. What newspaper ran the "Beautiful Baby Contest" on "All in the Family" (1971–80, CBS)?

3. Who played the title role in "Annie Oakley" (1953–56; syndicated)?

4. What was Bentley Gregg's phone number on "Bachelor Father" (1957–62, CBS, NBC, and ABC)?

5. Who played the evil Dr. Cassandra on "Batman" (1966–68, ABC)?

6. Who was Samantha's family doctor on "Bewitched" (1964–72, ABC)?

7. Where was the bus stop in "Bus Stop" (1961–62, ABC)?

8. Who played William Dante in "Dante" (1960–61, NBC)?

9. What sitcom did Eve Arden star in after "Our Miss Brooks" (1952–56, CBS)?

10. What airline did stewardess Lisa Benton (Connie Sellecca) work for on "Flying High" (1978–79, CBS)?

11. Who was the host of "Gangbusters" (1952, NBC)?

12. In what state was "Gibbsville" (1976, NBC)?

13. What was "The Skipper's" real name on "Gilligan's Island" (1964–67, CBS)?

14. Who played Mr. Angel on "Good Heavens" (1976, ABC)?

15. Who played the theme song on "The Green Hornet" (1966–67, ABC)?

16. Where did "Hec Ramsey" (1972–74, NBC) live?

17. Who sang the theme ("Seattle") from "Here Come the Brides" (1968–70, ABC)?

18. What Western did James Arness star in after "Gunsmoke" (1955–75, CBS)?

19. Who played Ben Richard's (Christopher George's) fianceé Sylvia on "The Immortal" (1970–71, ABC)?

20. Who played the title role in "Kentucky Jones" (1964–65, NBC)?

21. Who was Lassie's (1954–71, CBS) trainer?

22. Who played Elizabeth on "Life with Elizabeth" (1953–55; syndicated)?

23. Who played Betty Ramsey in "Lucy in Connecticut" (1960, CBS)?

24. Where did Walter Burnley (John McGiver) work on "Many Happy Returns" (1964–65, CBS)?

25. Who played Beauregard Maverick on "Maverick" (1957–62, ABC)?

26. Who played Colonel Edward McCauley on "Men into Space" (1959–60, CBS)?

27. Who played Michael Anthony on "The Millionaire" (1955–60, CBS)?

28. Who played "The Captain" (a Cagney role in the movies) on "Mr. Roberts" (1965–66, NBC)?

29. Who played Moses and Aaron in "Moses—The Lawgiver" (1975–79, CBS)?

30. On "My Three Sons" (1960–72, ABC and CBS) Fred MacMurray played a second role in addition to Steve Douglas. Who?

31. At what bank did Pearson Norby work in "Norby" (1955, NBC)?

32. Who played Jack Brennan in the adventure series "Paris 7000" (1970, ABC)?

33. Who played Rodney Harrington on "Peyton Place" (1964–69, ABC)?

34. Who played Dr. Jules Bedford's (Danny Thomas's) nurse Molly Gibbons on "The Practice" (1976–77, NBC)?

35. Who played Mrs. Helen Wilson on "Professional Father" (1955, CBS)?

36. In "The Pruitts of Southampton" (1966–67, ABC), what famous comedian played Mrs. Poindexter Pruitt?

37. At what school did Ray Milland teach in "The Ray Milland Show" (1953–55, CBS)?

38. What was the name of the riverboat on "Riverboat" (1959–61, NBC)?

39. What was the name of the houseboat on "The San Pedro Beach Bums" (1977, ABC)?

40. Who played the title role in "Sheena, Queen of the Jungle" (1955–56; syndicated)?

41. Who played Representative James Slattery on "Slattery's People" (1964–65, CBS)?

42. Who did Dick Smothers work for in "The Smothers Brothers Show" (1965–66, CBS)?

43. Who played the members of the singing group Sugar in "Sugar Time!" (1977–78, ABC)?

44. Who played Tracy Carlyle Hastings on "The Survivors" (1969–70, ABC)?

45. Who escorted passengers on the "Time Express" (1979, CBS)?

Answers on pages 246–247.

That was something, wasn't it? Well, we're going to give you a break, no matter how small it may seem. What we've done next is to take some of the more popular situation comedies to appear on your television screens over the years and compile a totally obscure mini-quiz for each one of them.

Much of the following information was collected by viewing the premiere episodes of the particular show. We found this to be absolutely fascinating! Seeing a premiere of a brand-new series is interesting enough, but to see a premiere of an established program with which you have a long association is terrific.

Most premieres lay the groundwork for future episodes on which to build. By watching the premieres well after you have become totally familiar with the series' progressions and characters, you can judge for yourself how well the groundwork was built upon. So get on your TV thinking caps and try and weasel through this next section.

## THE ADVENTURES OF OZZIE & HARRIET (1952–1966, ABC)

1. What type of cookie was Harriet preparing on the premiere episode?
2. Also on the premiere, what was the name of the girl who called David about going to a school dance?
3. Don Defor played the Nelsons' neighbor "Thorny." What was his wife's name? His son?
4. According to the premiere episode, how many girls did Thorny go steady with? How about Ozzie?

Answers on page 246.

## THE ANDY GRIFFITH SHOW (1960–1968, CBS)

1. What was the license plate number on Sheriff Andy Taylor's squad car?
2. In the episode "Barney Joins the Choir," what is the number (from the songbook) of the song the choir performed throughout the show?
3. How much was a ten-pound sack of potatoes at the local grocery store?

Answers on page 246.

## BEVERLY HILLBILLIES (1962–1971, CBS)

1. In what city was the oil company that bought the Clampett's swamp located?
2. How much was the original offer for the swamp, contingent on the amount of oil produced?
3. In the premiere episode, "The Clampetts Strike Oil," what did Granny cook for dinner?

4. What was the Clampetts' dog's name?

5. Jed asked if his favorite actor lived in Beverly Hills. Who was that actor?

Answers on page 246.

## BEWITCHED   (1964–1972, ABC)

1. In front of what building did Samantha first meet Darrin on the premiere episode?

2. When did Samantha tell Darrin she was a witch?

3. What state is Darrin from?

4. What does Samantha do to prove to Darrin that she's really a witch?

Answers on page 246.

## THE BOB NEWHART SHOW   (1972–1978, CBS)

1. When Bob finally agrees to go on vacation, where do the Hartleys go?

2. What is Bob's barber's name?

3. Mr. Peterson was played by veteran actor John Fiedler. What was Mrs. Peterson's first name on the series?

Answers on page 247.

## CAR 54, WHERE ARE YOU?   (1961–1963, ABC)

1. What stamp club was Muldoon a member of?

2. Which nightclub was described as "the fanciest place in the Bronx"?

3. What sign hung in the police locker room?

Answers on page 247.

## HERE'S LUCY   (1968–1974, CBS)

1. In the episode that featured both Elizabeth Taylor and Richard Burton, where did Richard Burton want to go but couldn't for fear he'd be recognized?

2. How did Richard Burton sneak out of his hotel without being recognized?

3. What did Lucy do to get in trouble in this episode?

Answers on page 247.

## I MARRIED JOAN   (1952–1955, NBC)

1. What did Joan do every Monday afternoon?

2. Where did Joan's friends give her a testimonial luncheon?

3. Who were the members of the Executive Council of the Ladies Club along with Joan?

4. In an episode titled "The St. Bernards," Joan is forbidden to buy a dog, yet by the show's end the Stevenses had two St. Bernards. What were their names?

Answers on page 247.

## JULIA   (1968–1971, NBC)

1. On the premiere episode, who interviewed Julia when she applied for a job?

2. What was Julia's apartment number? The Waggedorns'?

3. When Julia went on her job interview, she told Corey not to let anyone in the apartment. Corey did let Earl J. Waggedorn in. Why?

4. Julia didn't have a phone. From where did she make her phone calls?

5. Who played the role of television repairman Dick Privit on the premiere episode?

Answers on page 247.

## LEAVE IT TO BEAVER   (1957–1963, CBS and ABC)

1. What school did Beaver attend? Who was the school psychologist?

2. What did Beaver want to be when he grew up and why?

3. How much did Beaver pay for a haircut? Who was his regular barber?

4. What famous ballplayer did Beaver and his pals talk to on the phone?

Answers on page 247.

## THE MANY LOVES OF DOBIE GILLIS
(1959–1963, CBS)

1. What girl did both Dobie and Maynard fall for?

2. Why did Maynard leave the army?

3. What was the name of Dobie's father's business?

4. How much was a "Subgum Sundae" at the local soda fountain?

Answers on pages 247–248.

## THE MARY TYLER MOORE SHOW
(1970–1977, CBS)

1. Where did Ted and Georgette get married?

2. What color did Georgette wear at her wedding?

3. Who played the reverend that married Ted and Georgette and what was his name on the show?

4. What was Mary's religion?

5. According to the opening of the earliest episodes, what type of car did Mary drive to Minneapolis?

6. What is Ted's favorite Disney movie?

Answers on page 248.

## THE MUNSTERS (1964–1966, CBS)

1. What country club did Herman want to join?

2. How many wives did Grandpa have?

3. Herman was distraught when what TV show was cancelled?

Answers on page 248.

## MY THREE SONS (1960–1972, ABC and CBS)

1. In the premiere episode, what was the door-to-door salesman selling?

2. What second-grade classmate had a crush on Chip?

3. Also in the premiere episode, who did Steve date several times?

4. For how many years was Steve a widower?

5. What dessert did both "Bub" O'Casey and Steve's date make in the premiere episode?

Answers on page 248.

## THE PHIL SILVERS SHOW (1955–1959, CBS)

1. Who was Sergeant Bilko's girl friend? What was her hometown?

2. What was Sergeant Ruppert Ritzik's (Joe E. Ross) wife's name?

3. What sign hung in Bilko's room at the army base?

Answers on page 248.

## THE REAL McCOYS   (1957–1963, ABC and CBS)

1. How did the McCoys come to own their ranch in California?

2. When Grandpa Amos (Walter Brennen) first meets ranch foreman Pepino, what nationality does he think Pepino is?

3. Grandpa, in the premiere episode, says he was upset that Luke had married Kate. Whom did Grandpa want Luke to marry?

Answers on page 248.

## TOPPER   (1953–1956, CBS, ABC, and NBC)

1. In the premiere episode "Topper Meets the Kerbys," what number flight were the Kerbys taking to go on vacation?

2. How did the Kerbys meet their dog, Neil?

3. Who was Neil named after?

Answers on page 248.

# ABOUT
# THE
# AUTHORS

Fred Miranda was born and raised in Brooklyn, a place Ed Norton once described as the "garden spot of the U.S.A." Aside from being a devotee to 1960s television and trying to teach his parakeets dialogue from "The Honeymooners," Fred also writes music, loves sports, and is somewhat of a mediocre gourmet cook. His love for cooking, however, is equalled and surpassed by his love for eating!

Bill Ginch was born and raised in the shadow of the Bunker family in Queens, New York. Needless to say, Bill is also an avid fan of the great TV of yesteryear. He's also a collector of baseball memorabilia as well as being the owner of an ever expanding home video library. Bill is also hoping to use his skills as a cartoonist to develop a major character of his own that might signal a return to the great cartoons of years ago.

Fred and Bill are currently working on their second book, TV TRIVIA II, which will contain trivia questions and quizzes on Nighttime Soaps, TV Mini-Series, Made-for-TV Movies, Cartoons and much more.

# ANSWERS

## Doctor! Doctor!

### BEN CASEY

1. Casey was played by Vince Edwards.
2. Dr. Zorba was played by Sam Jaffe. He was replaced by Franchot Tone, who played Dr. Freeland.
3. Edwards was discovered by singer Bing Crosby.
4. Casey's brief encounter was with Stella Stevens, who played Jane Hancock. She had just come out of a 13-year coma.
5. Casey's other love interest was played by Bettye Ackerman.

### BREAKING POINT

1. Dr. Thompson was played by Paul Richards.
2. Thompson was known as "Dr. Mac."
3. Dr. Raymer was played by Edward Franz.

### CITY HOSPITAL

1. Dr. Crane was played by Melville Ruick.
2. Dr. Morrow was played by Ann Burr.
3. Along with "City Hospital" in this three-program package were "Crime Syndicated" and "Place the Face."

### DOC ELLIOTT

1. Elliott was played by James Franciscus.

2. He relocated to Gideon, Colorado.
3. His house calls were made either by plane or four-wheel-drive camper, medically equipped, of course.
4. Mags Brimble was played by Neva Patterson.
5. The producer was a real-life doctor, Sendor Stern, M.D.

## THE DOCTOR

"The Doctor" was Warner Anderson.

## DOCTORS' HOSPITAL

1. Dr. Goodwin was played by George Peppard.
2. He was Chief of Neurological Services.
3. Dr. Ortega was played by Victor Campos.

## DOCTORS' PRIVATE LIVES

1. They were both heart surgeons.
2. Dr. Wise was played by Ed Nelson; Dr. Latimer by John Gavin.

## DR. HUDSON'S SECRET JOURNAL

Dr. Hudson was played by John Howard.

## DR. KILDARE

1. Dr. Kildare was played by Richard Chamberlain.
2. Kildare's mentor, Dr. Gillespie, was played by Raymond Massey.
3. During the 1965–66 season, "Dr. Kildare" was aired twice a week as a half-hour show.
4. Dr. Agurski was played by Eddie Ryder; Dr. Gerson was played by Jud Taylor.
5. Some multi-week story lines ran for six episodes.

## DR. SIMON LOCKE

1. Dr. Locke was played by Sam Broom.
2. Dr. Sellers was played by Jack Albertson.
3. The title of the series was changed to "Police Surgeon."

## THE ELEVENTH HOUR

1. Dr. Bassett was played by Wendell Corey, and Dr. Graham was played by Jack Ging.
2. Dr. Starke, who replaced Dr. Bassett, was played by Ralph Bellamy.

### HAVING BABIES

1. The lead role was played by Susan Sullivan.
2. The new title was "Julie Farr, M.D."
3. Dr. Simmons was played by Mitchell Ryan.

### THE INTERNS

1. Dr. Goldstone was played by Broderick Crawford.
2. The actor who played Dr. Marsh, and later starred in "M*A*S*H," was Mike Farrell.

### JANET DEAN, REGISTERED NURSE

Janet Dean was played by Ella Rainer.

### THE LAZARUS SYNDROME

1. Dr. St. Clair was played by Louis Gossett, Jr.
2. He was Chief of Cardiology.
3. St. Clair's wife was played by Shiela Frazier.
4. Lazarus Syndrome refers to the patient's belief that doctors are godlike and capable of curing all illnesses.

### MATT LINCOLN

1. Vince Edwards, star of "Ben Casey," returned to play Matt Lincoln.
2. He ran a telephone-assistance service for troubled teenagers.
3. It was called Hotline.
4. Tag was played by Chelsea Brown.

### MEDIC

The role of Dr. Styner was played by Richard Boone.

### MEDICAL CENTER

1. Dr. Gannon was played by Chad Everett.
2. Dr. Lochner was played by James Daly.
3. Dr. Gannon also became director of the student health service.
4. Nurse Wilcox was efficiently played by Audrey Totter.
5. Nurse Chambers was played by Jayne Meadows.

### THE NEW DOCTORS

1. "The New Doctors" was part of "The Bold Ones."
2. The leading role was played by E. G. Marshall.
3. Dr. Hunter was played by David Hartman.

4. Dr. Stuart was played by John Saxon.
5. He specialized in heart transplants.

## NOAH'S ARK

1. The show dealt with veterinarians.
2. Dr. McCann was played by Paul Burke.
3. Dr. Rinehart was played by Vic Rodman.
4. The series was directed by Jack Webb.

## NURSE

1. Nurse Benjamin was played by Michael Learned.
2. Dr. Rose was played by Robert Reed.

## THE NURSES

1. The two nurses were played by Shirl Conway and Zina Bethune.
2. The series title was changed to "The Doctors and the Nurses."

## THE PSYCHIATRIST

1. "The Psychiatrist" was one element of "Four in One."
2. Dr. Whitman was played by Roy Thinnes.

## RAFFERTY

1. Dr. Rafferty was played by Patrick McGoohan.
2. Rafferty served as a doctor in the United States Army.

## WESTSIDE MEDICAL

The three doctors were played by James Sloyan, Linda Carlson, and Ernest Thompson, respectively.

## MATCHING (PAGE 12)

| | |
|---|---|
| 1. i | 7. g |
| 2. e | 8. b |
| 3. a | 9. k |
| 4. l | 10. f |
| 5. c | 11. h |
| 6. j | 12. d |

## MARCUS WELBY, M.D.

1. Dr. Welby was played by Robert Young.
2. Robert Young previously starred in "Father Knows Best."
3. Dr. Steven Kiley was played by James Brolin.
4. Consuelo's last name was Lopez and she was played by Elena Verdugo.

5. Dr. Welby had a practice in Santa Monica, California.
6. The Cleavers lived there in "Leave It to Beaver."
7. Dr. Kiley's brief love interest was Myra Lopez (1969–1970), and she was played by beautiful Anne Baxter.
8. Janet Blake was played by equally beautiful Pamela Hensley.
9. Dr. Welby's daughter's name was Sandy Porter (1975–1976).
10. The doctor's six-year-old grandson Phil (1975–1976) was played cutely by Gavin Brandan.

## ORDER IN THE COURT!

### ACCUSED

1. "Accused" was a spinoff of "Day in Court."
2. The presiding judge was played by Edgar Allen Jones, Jr., and he was a law professor.

### THE BLACK ROBE

1. The judge was played by Frank Thomas and the police officer by John Green.
2. The story lines came from cases tried in New York City's Police Night Court.

### THE D.A.

1. Deputy D.A. Paul Ryan was played by Robert Conrad, a veteran of seemingly countless television series.
2. Chief Deputy D.A. Stafford was played by Harry Morgan. His series nickname was "Staff."
3. The Public Defender's name was Katherine Benson. She was played by Julie Cobb.
4. Ned Romero played D.A. Investigator Bob Ramirez.

### THE DEFENDERS

1. Lawrence and Kenneth Preston were father and son.
2. Preston and Preston was the name of the firm they worked for.
3. Joan Miller was played by Joan Hackett.
4. The father was played by Ralph Bellamy, the son by William Shatner.

### HAWKINS

1. The lead role was played by James Stewart.

2. R. J. was played by Strother Martin, and he was Billy Jim's cousin.

## JUDD FOR THE DEFENSE

1. His full name was Clinton Judd.
2. Judd was played by Carl Betz.
3. Ben Caldwell was played by Stephen Young.

## JUSTICE

1. The story lines were based on files of cases taken from the National Legal Aid Society.
2. The series was produced by David Susskind.

## KATE McSHANE

1. Anne Meara, half of the very popular Stiller and Meara comedy team, starred as Kate McShane.
2. It was the first network dramatic series to feature a woman lawyer in the lead role.
3. Pat McShane was played by Sean McClory.

## THE LAW AND MR. JONES

1. His full name was Abraham Lincoln Jones, and he was played by James Whitmore.
2. C. E. Carruthers was played by Conlon Carter.

## THE LAWYERS

Walter Nichols was played by Burl Ives, Brian Darrell was played by Joseph Campanella, and Neil Darnell by James Farentino.

## LOCK-UP

1. Herbert L. Maris was played by MacDonald Carey.
2. "Casey" was played by Olive Carey.
3. There was no relationship between MacDonald Carey and Olive Carey.

## OWEN MARSHALL, COUNSELOR AT LAW

1. Owen Marshall was wonderfully played by Arthur Hill.
2. Jess Brandon was played by Lee Majors, who went on to fame as the Six Million Dollar Man.
3. Danny Paterno was played by Reni Santoni and Ted Warrick by David Soul.
4. Joan Darling starred as Frieda Krouse, Owen's loyal secretary.

5. Marshall was a widower in the series, but his 12-year-old daughter was played by Christine Matchett.
6. Marshall defended Steve Kiley, Marcus Welby's assistant, in a paternity suit.

## PETROCELLI

1. Petrocelli was played by Barry Newman.
2. Tony Petrocelli was a graduate of Harvard University.
3. Maggie Petrocelli was played by Susan Howard.
4. The Petrocellis lived in a camper-trailer unit.

## THE PUBLIC DEFENDER

1. Actor Reed Hadley created the role of the public defender.
2. A real public defender was saluted on each episode.

## ROSETTI AND RYAN

1. Frank Ryan was played by Squire Fridell and Joseph Rosetti by Tony Roberts.
2. Jessica Hornesby was played by Jane Elliot.
3. Before becoming a lawyer, Frank Ryan was a cop.

## SAM BENEDICT

Veteran actor Edmond O'Brien played the lead role.

## STOREFRONT LAWYERS

1. David Hansen was played by Robert Foxworth, Deborah Sullivan by Sheila Larkin, and Gabriel Kaye by David Arkin.
2. Hansen left the law firm of Horton, Troy, McNeil, Carroll and Clark.
3. The title was changed to "Men at Law."
4. The three went to work for Horton, Troy, McNeil, Carroll and Clark, the same firm David Hansen had left in the series's first episode.

## THEY STAND ACCUSED

1. Before the title changed, the series was called "Cross Question."
2. There were no scripts. Everything was ad lib.
3. Only the defendants and witnesses were actors. Everyone else, including lawyers, judges and jurors, were real-life lawyers, judges and jurors.
4. All the participants were briefed by William Wines, Assistant Attorney General of the State of Illinois.

## TRAFFIC COURT

The judge was Edgar Allen Jones, Jr., the bailiff was Frank Chandler McClure, and the court clerk was Samuel Whitson.

## TRIALS OF O'BRIEN

1. Daniel J. O'Brien was played by Peter Falk.
2. O'Brien's ex-wife, Katie, was played by Joanna Barnes.
3. She was simply known as "Miss G."
4. Dolph Sweet played Lieutenant Garrison.

## THE VERDICT IS YOURS

The court reporter was none other than Jim McKay, who went on to a fine career in sports broadcasting.

## WILLY

Willa Dodger was played by actress June Havoc.

## THE WITNESS

1. The series featured trials of old-time gangsters, such as Bugsy Siegel and Al Capone.
2. The court reporter was Verne Collett.

## MATCHING (page 21)

1. d
2. f
3. e
4. a
5. b
6. c

## PERRY MASON

1. Perry Mason was played by Raymond Burr.
2. Her name was Della Street, and she was played by actress Barbara Hale.
3. Paul Drake was played by William Hopper.
4. The series was created by novelist-lawyer Erle Stanley Gardner.
5. Yes. In 1963 his client refused to reveal certain evidence that would save her. Perry later set the record straight by proving his client was innocent and helping to locate the real guilty party.
6. The remake was titled "The New Adventures of Perry Mason."

7. The role of Perry Mason in "The New Adventures of Perry Mason" was played by Monte Markham.
8. Della was back, this time played by Sharon Acker.
9. Paul Drake was back too; this time he was played by Albert Statton.
10. In the original, Hamilton Burger was played by William Talman. In the remake, the role was played by Harry Guardino.

## How Intriguing!

### ASSIGNMENT VIENNA

1. "Assignment Vienna" was part of a multi-program package called "The Men."
2. Robert Conrad starred as Jake Webster.
3. Webster ran Jake's Bar & Grill in Vienna.
4. The series was filmed in Vienna, of course.
5. Major Caldwell was played by Charles Cioffi.

### THE AVENGERS

1. Jonathan Steed was played by Patrick Macnee.
2. The remake of "The Avengers" was called "The New Avengers."
3. Steed's first partner was Honor Blackman, from Bond-movie fame.
4. Diana Rigg played Emma Peel.
5. Tara was played by Linda Thorson.
6. Emma reunited with her long-lost husband and left the show.
7. "Mother" was played by Patrick Newell.

### THE BARON

1. "The Baron" was played by Steve Forrest.
2. He owned antique shops in London, Paris, and Washington, D.C.

### BEHIND CLOSED DOORS

Commander Matson was played by Bruce Gordon.

### BLUE LIGHT

1. David March was played by singer Robert Goulet.
2. The series was filmed in Germany.
3. The organization to which March belonged was called "Code—Blue Light."

## CASABLANCA

1. Rick Jason was played by Charles McCraw.
2. The club Rick owned was called Club American.

## CRUSADER

1. Matt Anders was played by actor Brian Keith.
2. He wanted to free the world's oppressed people from Communism and dictatorship. (Sounds like a Miss America contestant.)

## DANGER MAN

1. Danger Man John Drake was played by British actor Patrick McGoohan.
2. Danger Man was affiliated with N.A.T.O.

## DANGEROUS ASSIGNMENT

Steve Mitchell was played by Brian Donlevy, who also played the part on radio from 1950 to 1953.

## THE DELPHI BUREAU

1. Glenn Garth Gregory was played by Laurence Luckinbill.
2. Sybil Van Loween was played by Anne Jeffreys.

## DOORWAY TO DANGER

1. During its first season, this series was called "Door with No Name."
2. In 1951 Mel Ruick had the role; in 1952 it was played by Roland Winters, and finally by Raymond Bramley, in 1953.

## ESPIONAGE

This series was filmed throughout Europe.

## FIVE FINGERS

1. Victor Sebastian was played by David Hedison.
2. His code name was, of course, "Five Fingers."

## FOREIGN INTRIGUE

1. It was filmed in Europe, like so many other spy dramas.
2. Robert Cannon was played by Jerome Thor.
3. Michael Powers was played by James Daly.
4. Christopher Storm was played by Gerald Mohr.

## THE GIRL FROM U.N.C.L.E.

1. "The Girl from U.N.C.L.E." was a spinoff of "The Man from U.N.C.L.E."
2. Stefanie Powers played the lead role of April Dancer.
3. Leo G. Carroll played Alexander Waverly, U.N.C.L.E.'s organization head.

## HUNTER

1. James Hunter was played by James Franciscus.
2. His partner, Marty Shaw, was played by Linda Evans, who went on to fame in ABC's "Dynasty."
3. Ralph Bellamy, who played FDR in the movies, was Gerald Baker in this series.

## THE HUNTER

Bart Adams was played by Barry Nelson (1952–1954) and Keith Larsen (1954).

## I LED THREE LIVES

1. Herbert Philbrick was an average citizen, Communist Party member, and FBI counterspy.
2. Philbrick was played by Richard Carlson.
3. He was located in Boston.
4. Philbrick's wife, Eva, was played by Virginia Stefan.
5. The two agents were played by John Zaremba (Dressler) and Ed Hinton (Henderson).

## I SPY

1. Kelly Robinson was played by Robert Culp and Alexander Scott by comedian-turned-actor Bill Cosby.
2. It was the first time a black performer had a starring role in a dramatic series.
3. Robinson was a tennis pro, and Scott was his trainer.

## THE INVISIBLE MAN

1. No one knows. His identity was concealed by the series producers. He was only seen when he couldn't be seen.
2. Diane was his sister and Sally was his niece.

## IT TAKES A THIEF

1. Alexander Mundy was played by handsome Robert Wagner.
2. Mundy was a cat burglar.

3. He served time in San Jobel Prison.
4. Mundy's father, Alister, was played by none other than Fred Astaire.

## A MAN CALLED SLOANE

1. Robert Conrad played the lead role.
2. His full name was Thomas Remington Sloane III.
3. Torque was played by Ji-Tu Cumbuka.
4. The voice of "Effie" was Michele Carey.

## THE MAN CALLED X

Thurston was played by actor Barry Sullivan.

## THE MAN FROM U.N.C.L.E.

1. Napoleon Solo was played by Robert Vaughan and Illya Kuryakin by David McCallum.
2. Kuryakin was from Russia with love.
3. Lisa Rogers was played by Barbara Moore.

## THE MAN WHO NEVER WAS

1. Robert Lansing played Peter Murphy in this series.
2. Murphy assumed Wainwright's (his exact look-alike) identity after enemy agents had killed Wainwright thinking he was, in fact, Peter Murphy.
3. Eva Wainwright was played by actress Dana Wynter.

## PASSPORT TO DANGER

McQuinn was played by Cesar Romero.

## RENDEZVOUS

1. Nikki Angell was played by beautiful Ilona Massey.
2. Her nightclub was called "Chez Nikki."

## THE RHINEMANN EXCHANGE

1. This series was part of NBC's "Best Sellers."
2. The star of the series, in the role of David Spaulding, was Stephen Collins.
3. Leslie Hawkewood was played by Lauren Hutton.
4. This star-studded cast included Jose Ferrer (Rhinemannn), Vince Edwards (Swanson), Roddy McDowall (Ballard), Claude Akins (Kendall), and John Huston (Granville).

## THE SAINT

1. Handsome Roger Moore (007 in the movies) played sly Simon Templar.
2. The role of Templar in the remake was played by Ian Ogilvy.

## SECRET AGENT

The same actor played both John Drakes. Patrick McGoohan played the role in both "Danger Man" and "Secret Agent."

## SHADOW OF THE CLOAK

House was played by veteran movie actor Helmut Dantine.

## THE THIRD MAN

Lime was played by Michael Rennie, who had come to prominence in the motion picture "The Day the Earth Stood Still."

## GOOD GUYS AND BAD GUYS

1. Good Guys from "Mission Impossible"
2. Bad Guys from "A Man Called Sloane"
3. Even Worse Guys from "The Man From U.N.C.L.E."
4. Good Guys from "Danger Man"
5. Come on now, everybody knows this!
6. Good Guys from "A Man Called Sloane"
Did you make the right choices?

## MISSION IMPOSSIBLE

1. The role of James Phelps was played by Peter Graves.
2. Before Phelps came along, Steven Hill played the lead role of Daniel Briggs.
3. Martin Landau and Barbara Bain were regulars on the series, as Rollin Hand and Cinnamon Carter respectively.
4. Barney Collier was played by Greg Morris and Willie Armitage by Peter Lupus.
5. From 1970 to 1971 Lesley Ann Warren played Dana Lambert. From 1971 to 1973 Lynda Day George played Casey. From 1972 to 1973 Barbara Anderson was the lovely Mimi Davis.
6. None other than Leonard Nimoy played Paris.
7. "This tape will self-destruct in five seconds."
8. Barney Collier was an electronics expert.
9. Hand was a master of disguise.
10. The theme was written by Lalo Schiffrin.

## Hold on to Your Hats!

### THE AMERICAN GIRLS

1. Rebecca was played by Priscilla Barnes and Amy by Debra Clinger.
2. The girls were reporters for "The American Report," a TV news magazine.
3. The girls' home base was New York.

### BIG HAWAII

1. The Paradise Ranch served as the setting. It was owned by Barret Fears (John Dehner).
2. Mitch was played by Cliff Potts.

### THE BIONIC WOMAN

1. The Bionic Woman was Jaime Sommers, played by Lindsay Wagner.
2. Jaime was a tennis pro.
3. Jaime was born in Ojai, California.
4. The Bionic Woman worked for O.S.I. (Office of Scientific Information).

### BORN FREE

1. The series was filmed in East Africa.
2. George Adamson was played by Gary Collins, his wife by Diana Muldaur.
3. The lioness's name was Elsa.

### DAKTARI

1. Dr. Tracy was played by Marshall Thompson.
2. The series was filmed in Africa, USA, a wild animal habitat near Los Angeles.
3. It was a native word meaning "doctor."
4. Jenny was played by Erin Moran.

### THE GREEN HORNET

1. The Green Hornet was really Britt Reid, as played by Van Williams.
2. The Green Hornet drove a 1966 Crysler Imperial, which he called "Black Beauty."
3. Reid owned the *Daily Sentinel*.
4. Kato was played by Bruce Lee before he went on to fame with a career in martial arts films.

### THE IMMORTAL

1. "The Immortal" was race-driver Ben Richards, as played by Christopher George.
2. Antibodies in his blood made him immune to both disease and aging.
3. Maitland was played by David Brian.

### LUCAN

1. Lucan was played by Kevin Brophy.
2. Lucan was raised by wolves and in fact he had not associated with a human for his first ten years. "Lucan" refers to wolf.

### THE MAGICIAN

1. The magician was Anthony Blake, played by veteran Bill Bixby.
2. Pomeroy was played by Keene Curtis; he was a syndicated columnist.
3. The name of the plane was *The Spirit.*"

### THE MAN FROM ATLANTIS

1. Mark was the last survivor of Atlantis, as played by Patrick Duffy.
2. The experiments were done at the Foundation of Oceanic Research.
3. Dr. Merrill was played by lovely Belinda Montgomery.

### MR. LUCKY

1. Mr. Lucky was played by John Vivyan. He was a professional gambler.
2. The casino-ship was called *Fortuna.*
3. Andamo was played by Ross Martin.
4. "Mr. Lucky" was composed by Henry Mancini.

### MAYA

1. Terry Bowen was played by Jay North and Raji by Sajid Khan.
2. The series was filmed in India.
3. Maya was Raji's elephant.

### MOBILE ONE

1. Veteran of "Our Gang" fame, Jackie Cooper, played Campbell, a TV news reporter.
2. Campbell worked for KONE.

## THE NAME OF THE GAME

1. They all worked for Howard Publications in Los Angeles.
2. Glenn Howard was played by Gene Barry, Jeff Dillon by Tony Franciosa, and Dan Farrell by Robert Stack.

## THE NANCY DREW MYSTERIES

1. Nancy was played by Pamela Sue Martin.
2. Carson Drew, a criminal lawyer, played by William Schallert, was her father.
3. The Drews lived in River Heights, New York.
4. George was played by Jean Rasey (1977) and Susan Buckner (1977–78).

## THE PERSUADERS

1. The persuaders were Danny Wilde (Tony Curtis) and Lord Brett Sinclair (Roger Moore).
2. Judge Fulton (Laurence Naismith) invited the boys to a party and introduced them.

## ROUTE 66

1. Tod Stiles was played by Martin Milner and Buz Murdock (1960–1963) by George Maharis.
2. The boys rode in Tod's Corvette.
3. Linc Case (Glenn Corbett) replaced Buz Murdock in 1963.

## RUN FOR YOUR LIFE

1. Paul Bryan was played by Ben Gazzara.
2. Bryan was a lawyer before retiring.
3. Bryan had only two years to live and wanted to live the remainder of his life to the fullest.

## SEA HUNT

1. Nelson was played by Lloyd Bridges.
2. He became a free-lance undersea investigator.
3. His boat was called *The Argonaut*.

## THE SIX MILLION DOLLAR MAN

1. He was Steve Austin (Lee Majors), and he was an astronaut.
2. The surgery was performed by Dr. Rudy Wells (Alan Oppenheimer).

## THE SWISS FAMILY ROBINSON

1. Karl was played by Martin Milner, Lotte by Pat Delany.

2. The Robinsons had two kids, Fred (Willie Ames), and Ernie (Eric Olson).
3. Jean Lafitte made an appearance on the series.

### T.H.E. CAT

1. His real name was Thomas Hewitt Edward Cat.
2. T.H.E. Cat refused to carry a weapon.
3. The nightclub was in San Francisco. It was called the Casa del Gato.

### TARZAN

1. Tarzan was played by Ron Ely.
2. Jai, the orphan boy, was played by Manuel Padilla, Jr.

### THEN CAME BRONSON

1. Bronson was played by Michael Porter.
2. Bronson's change of life was brought on by the suicide of his best friend.

### 240-ROBERT

1. The three lead roles were Deputy Theodore Roosevelt Applegate III ("Trap"), played by John Bennett Perry; Deputy Dwayne Thibideaux, played by Mark Harmon; and Deputy Morgan Wainwright, played by Joanna Cassidy.
2. The three worked for the Emergency Detail Service (E.D.S.).

### MATCHING (PAGE 41)

| | | |
|---|---|---|
| 1. h | 6. k | 11. o |
| 2. d | 7. a | 12. j |
| 3. m | 8. f | 13. c |
| 4. e | 9. b | 14. l |
| 5. i | 10. g | 15. n |

### BATMAN

1. The series was set in Gotham City.
2. Batgirl was librarian Barbara Gordon. She was played by Yvonne Craig.
3. Bruce Wayne (Adam West) lived at courtly Wayne Manor.
4. She was Aunt Harriet Cooper. He was Alfred Pennyworth.
5. The secret passage was activated by lifting the head of the bust near the secret door and pressing a button, of course.

6. The Catwoman was played by Eartha Kitt, Julie Newmar, and Lee Meriweather.
7. Mr. Freeze was played by Walter Slezak and Otto Preminger. The Riddler by John Astin and Frank Gorshin.
8. Bruce Wayne's parents were murdered. He was raised by Alfred.
9. Robin's real name was Dick Grayson (played by Burt Ward).
10. Commissioner Gordon was played by Neil Hamilton and Chief O'Hara by Stafford Repp.
11. The Batphone was bright red.
12. The Archer was Art Carney, The Black Widow was Tallulah Bankhead, The Bookworm was Roddy McDowall, Egghead was Vincent Price, The Joker was Cesar Romero, King Tut was Victor Buono, Lola Lasagna was Ethel Merman, Louie the Lilac was Milton Berle, The Mad Hatter was David Wayne, The Penguin was Burgess Meredith, Shame was Cliff Robertson, and the Siren was beautiful Joan Collins.

## SUPERMAN

1. Superman's real name was Kal-El, and he was played by George Reeves.
2. Superman came from the planet Krypton.
3. Superman's parents were Jor-El and Lara, played by Robert Rockwell and Aline Towne.
4. The rocket carrying Superman landed in the town of Smallville.
5. Superman was raised by a couple named Eben and Sarah Kent.
6. "Superman on Earth" was the name of the pilot episode.
7. Superman was known as Clark Kent and worked as a reporter for *The Daily Planet*.
8. Perry White, played by John Hamilton, was the chief editor of *The Daily Planet*. He would often shout "Great Caesar's Ghost!"
9. Lois Lane, played by Phyllis Coates and Noel Neill,** and Jimmy Olsen, played by Jack Larson, were the two young reporters who also worked at *The Daily Planet*.
10. Kryptonite was the only thing that could harm Superman. These were fragments of rock that fell to Earth when Superman's planet (Krypton) exploded.
11. The little girl was played by Kathy Williams, and she wanted Superman to take her to the county fair.
12. Her doll recited "Mary Had a Little Lamb."

*"Stamp Day for Superman" was never shown on TV but used as a promo to promote the hobby of U.S. stamp collecting for children.
**Noel Neill had a cameo role in the motion picture *Superman*.

## STOP IN THE NAME OF THE LAW!

### ADAM 12

1. Martin Milner and Kent McCord played the roles of Officer Pete Malloy and Officer Jim Reed.
2. Officers Malloy and Reed were members of the Los Angeles Police Department.
3. Jack Webb was the producer of "Adam 12."

### AMY PRENTISS

1. Amy Prentiss was played by Jessica Walter.
2. She worked at the San Francisco Police Department as Chief of Detectives.
3. She was a widow with a daughter played by Helen Hunt.

### BARETTA

1. The hotel was run by Billy Truman, played by Tom Ewell.
2. "Keep Your Eye on the Sparrow" was the theme song, which was sung by Sammy Davis, Jr.

### THE BLUE KNIGHT

Bumper Morgan was known as the Blue Knight and was played by George Kennedy.

### CADE'S COUNTY

1. Sam Cade was played by Glenn Ford.
2. Madrid County, California, was the setting for this Western/police drama.
3. One of Cade's young deputies was played by Peter Ford (Glenn's son), who played Pete.

### CHIPS

1. CHIPS stood for California Highway Patrol.
2. Officer Jon Baker was played by Larry Wilcox, and Officer Frank "Ponch" Poncherello was played by Eric Estrada.
3. Harlan was the police mechanic and was played by Lou Wagner.

### CHOPPER ONE

Officer Don Burdick was played by Jim McMullan, and Officer Gil Foley was played by Dirk Benedict.

## COLUMBO

1. Peter Falk played Lieutenant Columbo of the L.A.P.D.
2. Columbo always wore a dirty old raincoat.
3. Columbo never did have a first name on the series.

## DAN AUGUST

Dan August was played by Burt Reynolds, who was Detective Lieutenant of Homicide.

## DELVECCHIO

1. Sergeant Dominick Delvecchio was played by Judd Hirsch, and he fought crime in the city of Los Angeles.
2. Delvecchio's partner was Sergeant Paul Shonski and was played by Charles Haid. Their boss was Lieutenant Macavan, played by Michael Conrad.
3. Delvecchio's father's name was Tomaso, played by Mario Gallo, who ran a local barbershop.

*Note of interest: Charles Haid and Michael Conrad later teamed up again on a more successful police series by the name of "Hill Street Blues."

## DRAGNET

1. Sergeant Joe Friday was played by Jack Webb and his partner, Officer Bill Gannon, was played by Harry Morgan.
2. The director of "Dragnet" was also the star, Jack Webb.
3. Sergeant Friday's badge number was 714.

## EISCHIED

1. Eischied was played by Joe Don Baker, who worked for the New York City Police.
2. Eischied's companion was his pet cat, called P. C.

## THE F.B.I.

1. Efrem Zimbalist, Jr., portrayed Inspector Lewis Erskine.
2. Arthur Ward, portrayed by Philip Abbot, was the assistant to the F.B.I. director.
3. F.B.I. Director J. Edgar Hoover gave his cooperation for the filming of this TV show.

## HAWAII FIVE-O

1. Jack Lord portrayed Detective Steve McGarrett.
2. James MacArthur played Detective Danny Williams, who was the assistant to McGarrett.

3. Philip Grey, played by Richard Denning, was the Governor of Hawaii.
4. Wo Fat, played by Khigh Dhiegh, was one of Hawaii's most wanted men.

## HIGHWAY PATROL

Broderick Crawford portrayed Chief Don Matthews.

## IRONSIDE

1. Raymond Burr played Robert Ironside, Chief of Detectives for the San Francisco Police Department.
2. Don Mitchell played Mark Singer, Ironside's bodyguard.
3. A bullet was lodged near his spine and left him paralyzed from the waist down.

## JOE FORRESTER

Joe Forrester was played by Lloyd Bridges, and his girl friend was played by Patricia Crowley.

## KOJAK

1. Telly Savalas played Lieutenant Theo Kojak.
2. Kojak worked for the 13th Precinct in Manhattan.
3. Kojak's famous trademark was the lollipop.

## LANIGAN'S RABBI

Art Carney played Paul Lanigan, Chief of Police for a small California town.

## M SQUAD

Lee Marvin played Lieutenant Frank Ballinger, who also served as the narrator.

## MADIGAN

Richard Widmark played Don Madigan, who was a police detective for the New York Police Department.

## McCLOUD

1. Dennis Weaver played Sam McCloud, who came to New York from Taos, New Mexico.
2. McCloud worked at the 27th Precinct in Manhattan.
3. Diana Muldaur played Chris Coughlin, McCloud's seldom seen girl friend, who worked as a writer.

## McMILLAN AND WIFE

1. Rock Hudson portrayed San Francisco Police Commissioner Stewart McMillan.
2. Susan Saint Jamess played Sally McMillan.
3. Nancy Walker played the McMillans' maid, Mildred.

## MOD SQUAD

1. The three members of the Mod Squad were Pete Cochran, played by Michael Cole; Linc Hayes, played by Clarence Williams III; and Julie Barnes, played by Peggy Lipton.
2. Captain Adam Greer, played by Tige Andrews, was the one responsible for originating the Mod Squad.
3. The trio used a station wagon called "Woody" to get around town.

## N.Y.P.D.

The three main stars were Detective Lieutenant Mike Haines, played by Jack Warden; Detective Jeff Ward, played by Robert Hooks; and Detective Johnny Carso, played by Frank Converse.

## NAKED CITY

"There are 8 million stories in the Naked City."

## POLICE WOMAN

1. Angie Dickinson played Sergeant Suzanne "Pepper" Anderson.
2. Sergeant Pepper Anderson worked on the vice squad for L.A.P.D.

## THE ROOKIES

1. Sam Melville played Officer Mike Danko, and his wife, Jill, was played by Kate Jackson.
2. Gerald S. O'Loughlin played Lieutenant Eddie Ryker.
3. Mike Danko's wife, Jill, worked as a registered nurse.

## S.W.A.T.

1. S.W.A.T. stood for Special Weapons and Tactics.
2. Steve Forrest was commanding officer Lieutenant Don "Hondo" Harrelson.

## STARSKY & HUTCH

1. Paul Michael Glaser played Starsky, and David Soul played Hutch.
2. Bernie Hamilton was their boss, Captain Harold Dobey.
3. They drove around in a red souped-up Ford Torino.

## STREETS OF SAN FRANCISCO

1. Karl Malden played Detective Stone, who worked for the San Francisco Police Department.
2. Detective Stone's original partner was Steve Keller, played by Michael Douglas, who was later replaced by Richard Hatch, who played Inspector Don Robbins.

## TOMA

1. Tony Musante played Detective David Toma on this show, which was based on the real-life doings of this Newark, New Jersey Police Officer.
2. Simon Oakland played Toma's boss Inspector Spooner.

## MATCHING # 1 (PAGES 53—54)

| | | |
|---|---|---|
| 1. k | 6. o | 11. l |
| 2. e | 7. b | 12. f |
| 3. g | 8. i | 13. n |
| 4. j | 9. h | 14. d |
| 5. a | 10. c | 15. m |

## MATCHING #2 (PAGE 54)

| | | |
|---|---|---|
| 1. l | 6. m | 11. e |
| 2. f | 7. c | 12. h |
| 3. g | 8. i | 13. j |
| 4. a | 9. d | 14. n |
| 5. o | 10. k | 15. b |

## THE UNTOUCHABLES

1. The series' narrator was Walter Winchell.
2. Eliot Ness was played by Robert Stack.
3. The Ness character was based on real-life crime fighter Eliot Ness.
4. "The Untouchables" was a name tagged on Ness's band of agents.
5. a) Frank Nitti was played by Bruce Gordon.
   b) Jake Guzik was played by Nehemiah Persoff.
   c) Al Capone was played by Neville Brand.
   d) Bugs Moran was played by Lloyd Nolan.
   e) Mad Dog Coll was played by Clu Gulager.

## PUT THE WAGONS IN A CIRCLE!

### BAT MASTERSON

1. Bat Masterson was played by Gene Barry.

2. Bat always wore a derby hat and carried a gold-topped cane.
3. The series' locale was Tombstone, Arizona.

## THE BIG VALLEY

1. Victoria Barkley was played by the legendary Barbara Stanwyck.
2. Jarrod was played by Richard Long, Nick by Peter Breck, Heath by Lee Majors, and beautiful Audra by equally beautiful Linda Evans.

## BRANDED

1. Chuck Connors starred as Jason McCord.
2. .Jason McCord graduated from West Point.

## BROKEN ARROW

1. Michael Ansara played Apache chief, Cochise.
2. Tom Jeffords was played by John Lupton.

## CHEYENNE

1. Cheyenne Brodie was played by Clint Walker.
2. Cheyenne's sidekick was Smitty.

## CIMARRON STRIP

1. The Cimarron Strip was a border between the Kansas and Indian territories.
2. Crown was played by Stuart Whitman.

## DANIEL BOONE

1. Daniel Boone was played by Fess Parker.
2. Cooper was played by Roosevelt Grier.

## DEATH VALLEY DAYS

1. The hosts were Stanley Andrews (1952–1965), Ronald Reagan (1965–1966), Robert Taylor (1966–1968), Dale Robertson (1968–1972), and Merle Haggard (1975).
2. Twenty Mule Team Borax was the major sponsor.

## HAVE GUN WILL TRAVEL

1. Paladin was played by Richard Boone.
2. Paladin stayed at the Hotel Carlton.

## HIGH CHAPARRAL

1. High Chaparral was a ranch owned by Big John Cannon (Leif Erickson).
2. Buck was played by Cameron Mitchell.

## HOTEL DE PAREE

1. The Hotel De Paree was in Georgetown, Colorado.
2. Sundance was played by Earl Holliman.

## THE LAWMAN

1. The Lawman was Marshal Dan Troop, played by John Russell.
2. Deputy McKay was played by Peter Brown.

## THE LIFE AND LEGEND OF WYATT EARP

1. Wyatt Earp was played by Hugh O'Brien.
2. Masterson was played by Mason Alan Dinehart III.

## THE LONE RANGER

1. Both Clayton Moore (1949–1952) and John Hart (1952–1954) played the Lone Ranger.
2. Tonto was played by Jay Silverheels.

## MAVERICK

1. Bret was played by James Garner and Bart by Jack Kelly.
2. Buckley was played by Efrem Zimbalist, Jr.

## THE MONROES

1. There were five Monroe children, aged 6 to 18.
2. Their names were (youngest to oldest) Amy and Fennimore (twins), Jefferson, Kathy and Clayt.

## OVERLAND TRAIL

1. William Bendix was cast as Kelly.
2. Flippen was played by Doug McClure.

## RAWHIDE

1. Yates was played by superstar Clint Eastwood.
2. The trail boss was Gil Favor. He was played by Eric Fleming.

## THE RIFLEMAN

1. The setting was a town called North Fork, New Mexico.

2. Lucas was played by Chuck Connors and Mark by Johnny Crawford. They were father and son.

## SHANE

1. Shane was played by David Carradine.
2. The final line, spoken by Brandon DeWilde, was "Shane . . . come back!"

## THE VIRGINIAN

1. "The Virginian" was played by James Drury.
2. Shiloh Ranch was the setting for the series.

## WAGON TRAIN

1. Major Seth Adams (1957–1961) was played by Ward Bond and Flint McCollough (1957–1962) by Robert Horton.
2. The wagon train always started at St. Joseph, Missouri.

## WANTED: DEAD OR ALIVE

1. John Randall was played by Steve McQueen.
2. His sidekick, Jason Nichols (1960), was played by Wright King.

## THE WILD, WILD WEST

1. West served under President Grant.
2. West was played by Robert Conrad and Gordon by Ross Martin.
3. Michael Dunn played the evil Dr. Miguelito Loveless.

## ZORRO

1. Zorro's real name was Don Diego de la Vega.
2. Zorro was played by Guy Williams.
3. Bernardo was a deaf-mute.

## ALIAS SMITH AND JONES

1. Heyes was played by Peter Duel (1971–1972) and then by Roger Davis (1972–1973).
2. Curry was played by Ben Murphy.
3. Hale was played by Sally Field.
4. Roger Davis was first the series narrator in 1971–1972.

## KUNG FU

1. Kung Fu wasn't a character. It is a form of martial art.
2. Carradine starred as Kwai Chang Caine. He came to America after killing a member of the Chinese royal family. When in America, he began an exhaustive search for his brother.

3. Caine was taught by Master Po and Master Kan.
4. Caine's character, in his youth, was played by Radames Pera.

MATCHING # 1 (PAGES 63—64)

| | |
|---|---|
| 1. c | 4. b |
| 2. e | 5. a |
| 3. f | 6. d |

MATCHING # 2 (PAGE 64)

| | | |
|---|---|---|
| 1. h | 6. a | 11. k |
| 2. j | 7. l | 12. e |
| 3. d | 8. c | 13. b |
| 4. i | 9. f | 14. g |
| 5. m | 10. o | 15. n |

MATCHING # 3 (PAGE 65)

| | | |
|---|---|---|
| 1. e | 6. l | 11. g |
| 2. i | 7. f | 12. n |
| 3. o | 8. c | 13. d |
| 4. a | 9. k | 14. m |
| 5. h | 10. j | 15. b |

GUNSMOKE

1. The series locale was Dodge City, Kansas.
2. "Miss Kitty" owned the Longbranch Saloon.
3. His name was Dr. Galen Adams. He was played by Milburn Stone.
4. Chester Goode (1955–1964) was played by Dennis Weaver and Festuss Haggen (1964–1975) by Ken Curtis.
5. Asper was played by Burt Reynolds.

BONANZA

1. Adam (1959–1965) was played by Pernell Roberts, "Hoss" (1959–1972) by Dan Blocker, and Little Joe by Michael Landon.
2. The cook, Hop Sing, was played by Victor Sen Yung.
3. Candy was played by David Canary.
4. Reruns were shown under the title "Ponderosa."
5. The theme song was called "Bonanza."

# STAKE-OUT!

## BANACEK

1. Thomas Banacek was played by George Peppard.
2. The series was set in Boston.

## BANYON

1. Banyon charged $20 a day, no matter what.
2. Banyon was played by Robert Forster.

## BRONK

1. Jack Palance played Lieutenant Alex Bronkov.
2. Bronk took place in Ocean City, California.
3. She died in an auto accident, in which Bronk's daughter became a cripple.

## BURKE'S LAW

1. Burke was played by Gene Barry.
2. The chauffeur's name was Henry, and he drove a Rolls-Royce.
3. "Amos Burke—Secret Agent" was how the series was known in its last season.

## CANNON

1. Cannon worked in Los Angeles.
2. He was played by portly William Conrad.
3. He drove a black Continental convertible.

## CHARLIE'S ANGELS

1. The original three angels were Sabrina Duncan (Kate Jackson), Jill Monroe (Farrah Fawcett-Majors) and Kelly Garrett (Jaclyn Smith). Later angels were Kris Monroe (Cheryl Ladd), Tiffany Welles (Shelly Hack), and Julie Rogers (Tanya Roberts).
2. Charlie's "voice" was John Forsythe. His full name was Charlie Townsend.
3. David Doyle played John Bosley, middleman between Charlie and the angels.

## CITY OF ANGELS

1. Axminster was played by Wayne Rogers.
2. Marsha was played by Elaine Joyce.

## COOL MILLION

1. Keyes was an ex-CIA agent played by James Farentino.
2. Keyes routinely charged a million dollars for his services.

## FARADAY AND COMPANY

1. He was innocent and released after being wrongly held for 25 years.
2. Steve Faraday's mother was Frank's secretary Lou Carson.

## GRIFF

1. Wade Griffin was played by Lorne Greene.
2. The name was simply Wade Griffin Investigations.
3. He was on the police force for 30 years before he resigned over a matter of principle.

## HARRY-O

1. Harry Orwell was played by David Janssen.
2. Harry moved from San Diego to Santa Monica.
3. Harry's neighbor was Farrah Fawcett.

## HAWAIIAN EYE

1. Lopaka was played by Robert Conrad and Steel by Anthony Eisley.
2. Their base of operations was the Hawaiian Village Hotel.
3. Cricket was played by bouncy Connie Stevens.

## HONEY WEST

1. Honey West was played by Anne Francis.
2. Her lipstick was a radio transmitter.
3. Her office was a van marked "H. W. Bolt & Co., TV Service."

## KAZ

1. His full name was Martin "Kaz" Kazinsky. He was played by Ron Liebman.
2. Kaz worked for the law firm of Bennett, Rheinhart, and Alquist.
3. He lived over the Sterling Gate, a jazz club.
4. He earned his law degree while in prison.

## LONGSTREET

1. Mike Longstreet, played by James Franciscus, was blind.
2. Pax was a white German shepherd guide dog.
3. Longstreet had an electronic cane that judged distances.
4. Longstreet's self-defense instructor was none other than Bruce Lee.

## THE MANHUNTER

1. Barrett was played by Ken Howard.
2. His farm was in Idaho.

## MANNIX

1. Mike Conners played Mannix, who originally worked for Intertect, a detective firm.
2. Peggy was played by Gail Fisher.

## MATT HELM

1. Helm was played here by Tony Franciosa.
2. Claire Kronski was played by Loraine Stephens.

## McCOY

1. McCoy was played by veteran movie actor Tony Curtis.
2. Gideon Gibbs was played by Roscoe Lee Browne. He made his living as a nightclub comedian.

## THE MOST DEADLY GAME

1. Jonathan Croft was played by George Maharis.
2. Vanessa Smith was played by Yvette Mimieux and Mr. Arcane by Ralph Bellamy.

## 77 SUNSET STRIP

1. Bailey was played by Efrem Zimbalist, Jr., and Spencer by Roger Smith.
2. Gerald Lloyd Kookson III was known by the nickname "Kookie."
3. Dino's restaurant was located next door.

## SHAFT

1. Shaft was played by Richard Roundtree.
2. The series locale was New York City.
3. Barth played the role of Lieutenant Al Rossi.

## THE SNOOP SISTERS

1. Ernesta Snoop was played by Helen Hayes, Gwen Snoop by Mildred Natwick.
2. The Snoop sisters were successful mystery writers.
3. Lieutenant Ostrowski was the Snoop sisters' nephew. He was played by Bert Convy.

## SWITCH

1. Peter Ryan was the ex-con played by Robert Wagner, and Frank McBride was the ex-cop played by Eddie Albert.
2. The series was based in Los Angeles.
3. Maggie was played by pretty Sharon Gless.

## TENAFLY

1. James McEachin played Harry Tenafly. He lived in Los Angeles with his family.
2. Ruth Tenafly was played by Lillian Lehman.

## MATCHING (PAGE 74)

| | |
|---|---|
| 1. g | 6. j |
| 2. d | 7. i |
| 3. h | 8. c |
| 4. b | 9. f |
| 5. a | 10. e |

## THE THIN MAN

1. Nick and Nora Charles were played by Peter Lawford and Phyllis Kirk, respectively.
2. Asta was a wire-haired fox terrier.
3. The Charleses lived in Manhattan, on Park Avenue.
4. He regularly helped sniff out clues and capture suspects.
5. Nick and Nora were the creation of Dashiell Hammett.
6. Beatrice Dane used the name "Blondie Collins" as an alias. She was played by Nita Talbot.

## OUT OF THIS WORLD!

### BATTLESTAR GALACTICA

1. Lorne Greene played Commander Adama, and Richard Hatch played his son, Captain Apollo.
2. The half-human robot villains that pursued the *Galactica* were called Cylons.
3. "Battlestar Galactica" was retitled "Galactica 1980."

### BEYOND WESTWORLD

Westworld was an amusement park where visitors could live out their wildest fantasies. The park was full of robots that looked and acted like real people.

## BUCK ROGERS

1. Ken Dibbs and Robert Pastene both played Buck Rogers.
2. Lou Prentis played Wilma Deering.

## BUCK ROGERS IN THE 25TH CENTURY

1. Buck Rogers was played by Gil Gerard.
2. Dr. Huer was played by Tim O'Connor.
3. Twiki was the name of the robot aide, given to Buck.

## FLASH GORDON

1. Flash Gordon was played by Steve Holland.
2. Flash Gordon's companions were Dale Arden, played by Irene Champlin, and Dr. Zharkov, played by Joe Nash.
3. Flash and his two friends had set off for the planet Mongo.
4. The Emperor of Mongo was the destructive Ming.

## THE INVADERS

1. David Vincent was played by Roy Thinnes.
2. David Vincent was an architect.
3. Knowing who were the Invaders was not hard. White Invaders could not bend their pinky fingers, and Black Invaders had all-black palms.

## LOGAN'S RUN

1. The role of Logan was played by Gregory Harrison.
2. Logan was running from the City of Domes.
3. The reason why Logan was running was because people couldn't live past their thirtieth birthday, and Logan's thirtieth birthday was very near.

## OUTER LIMITS

"There is nothing wrong with your TV set. We are controlling transmission. We control the vertical and the horizontal. For the next hour we will control all that you see and hear and think. You are watching a drama that reaches from the inner mind to the Outer Limits."

## PLANET OF THE APES

1. The two astronauts were Alan Virdon, played by Ron Harper, and Pete Burke, played by James Naughton.
2. Galen was played by Roddy McDowall, who recreated the role he played in the motion picture of the same name.

## SPACE: 1999

1. The cast was headed by husband-and-wife stars Martin Landau and Barbara Bain.
2. Koenig's mentor was Professor Victor Bergman, played by Barry Morse.
3. Maya was the alien from the planet Psychon who could transform herself into various forms of life.
4. Moonbase Alpha was located on the surface of the Moon.

## STAR TREK

1. The Klingons and Romulans were the two alien races that appeared throughout the show to confront our heroes.
2. Captain James T. Kirk was played by William Shatner, and he was commander of the starship U.S.S. *Enterprise*.
3. The chief engineer was Lieutenant Commander Montgomery Scott, played by James Doohan. He was called simply "Scotty."
4. The ship's doctor was Dr. Leonard McCoy, played by DeForest Kelley. His nickname was "Bones."
5. Mr. Spock was played by Leonard Nimoy. His father was Vulcan, and his mother was an Earth woman; this gave him the distinction of being a half-breed.

## THE TWILIGHT ZONE

1. Rod Serling was the host.
2. "You unlock this door with the key of imagination. Beyond it is another dimension. A dimension of sound. A dimension of sight. A dimension of mind. You're moving into a land of both shadow and substance...of things and ideas.... You've just crossed over...into the Twilight Zone."
3. The episode was called "The Invaders" and starred Agnes Moorhead.
4. Mr. Death was played by Robert Redford.
5. a. "Kick the Can"
   b. "It's a Good Life"
   c. "Nightmare at 20,000 Feet"

## UFO

1. The show was set in the year 1980.
2. Shado stood for Supreme Headquarter Alien Defense Organization.
3. Its commander was Edward Straker, played by Ed Bishop.

## VOYAGE TO THE BOTTOM OF THE SEA

1. The submarine was called *Seaview*, and the minisub that could fly through the air was called *The Flying Fish*.
2. Admiral Harriman Nelson was played by Richard Basehart.
3. Admiral Nelson was Director of the Nelson Institute of Marine Research, at Santa Barbara, California.
4. Lee Crane was the Commander of the *Seaview* and was played by David Hedison.
5. Chip Morton was the Lieutenant Commander and was played by Robert Dowdell.
6. *The Vulcan* was the enemy submarine in "The Lost Bomb."

## LOST IN SPACE

1. The family lost in space were the Robinsons.
2. The Robinson family traveled in the *Jupiter II*.
3. The pilot episode was named "The Reluctant Stowaway."
4. The Robinsons took off in the year 1997.
5. The family became lost in space due to sabotage by Dr. Zachary Smith, played by Jonathan Harris.
6. The pilot of the *Jupiter II* was Major Don West, played by Mark Goddard.
7. There were five members of the Robinson family. Professor John Robinson was played by Guy Williams. His wife, Maureen, was played by June Lockhart. Their three children were Judy, played by Marta Kristen; Penny, played by Angela Cartwright; and Will, played by Billy Mumy.
8. The voice of the robot was supplied by Bob May.

## THE TIME TUNNEL

1. The two scientists were Dr. Tony Newman, played by James Darren, and Dr. Doug Phillips, played by Robert Colbert.
2. Tony and Doug first found themselves aboard the *Titanic*.
3. The two associates were Dr. Anna MacGregor, played by Lee Meriweather, and Dr. Raymond Swain, played by John Zaremba.
4. The Time Tunnel was located below the Arizona desert.
5. In the episode "The Day the Sky Fell Down," we find out that Tony was born at Pearl Harbor.

## LAND OF THE GIANTS

1. It was 1983 when the show first started.
2. The flight plan was to take seven people from Los Angeles to London.
3. The spaceship was called the *Spindrift*.

4. Captain Steve Burton, played by Gary Conway, was the pilot, and Dan Erikson, played by Don Marshall, was the co-pilot.
5. The first episode was called "The Crash."

## WHICH WAY TO THE FRONT?

### THE AMERICANS

1. "The Americans" dealt with the Civil War.
2. The two brothers were Ben and Jeff Canfield.
3. The boys grew up in Harper's Ferry, Virginia.

### BAA BAA BLACK SHEEP

1. Conrad played Major Gregory "Pappy" Boyington.
2. The series reappeared as "Black Sheep Squadron."
3. Lord was played by Dana Elcar, and Gutterman by James Whitmore.

### COMBAT

1. Hanley was played by Rick Jason, and Saunders by Vic Morrow.
2. The fighting took place in Europe.
3. Braddock was played by comedian Shecky Green.

### COMBAT SERGEANT

1. Sergeant Nelson was played by Michael Thomas.
2. The series was set in North Africa.

### CONVOY

1. Commander Talbot was played by John Gavin.
2. Talbot was stationed aboard U.S. Navy Destroyer Escort *DD 181*.
3. Foster's freighter was called the *Flagship*.

### FROM HERE TO ETERNITY

1. The series was set in Hawaii, 1941.
2. Natalie Wood (1979) and Barbara Hershey (1980) both played Karen Holmes.
3. Major Holmes was played by Roy Thinnes.

### THE GALLANT MEN

1. The series was set in Italy.
2. The infantry division chronicled was the 36th Infantry ("Texas") Division.

## JERICHO

a. Shepard was a captain in American Army Intelligence.
b. Andre was an officer in the Free French Air Force.
c. Gage was a lieutenant in the British Navy.

## O.S.S.

1. O.S.S. stood for the Office of Strategic Services, an actual World War II spy agency.
2. After the war, the O.S.S. was replaced by the C.I.A.
3. "The Chief" was played by Lionel Murton.

## ONCE AN EAGLE

1. The series was set during World War I.
2. Sam Damon was played by Sam Elliott, and Courtney Massengale by Cliff Potts.

## THE RAT PATROL

1. "The Rat Patrol" was set in North Africa early on in World War II.
2. The series was filmed in Spain.
3. The four men were Sergeant Sam Troy (Chris George), Sergeant Jack Moffitt (Gary Raymond), Private Mark Hitchcock (Lawrence Casey), and Private Tully Pettigrew (Justin Tar).
4. They drove two jeeps mounted with machine guns.

## TWELVE O'CLOCK HIGH

1. Savage was played by Robert Lansing.
2. Colonel Joe Gallagher (Paul Burke) took command after the untimely death of Savage.
3. They commanded the 918th Bombardment Group of the U.S. Eighth Air Force.

## THE WACKIEST SHIP IN THE ARMY

1. It was a twin-masted schooner presented to the U.S. by New Zealand.
2. The ship was called the *Kiwi*.
3. Major Butcher was played by Jack Warden, and Lieutenant Riddle by Gary Collins.

## GARRISON'S GORILLAS

1. They were recruited by the army from prisons in the U.S.
2. The action was from World War II.

3. They were promised a pardon if they did well.
4. The Gorillas were Actor, Casino, Goniff, and Chief.
5. Garrison was played by Ron Harper.
6. They were based in England.

## Generally Speaking . . .

### APPLE'S WAY

1. The series took place in Appleton, Iowa.
2. George Apple, the architect, was played by Ronny Cox.
3. The Apples previously lived in Los Angeles.
4. Patricia was played by Franny Michel (1974) and Kristy McNichol (1974–1975).
5. She was played by an unknown Farrah Fawcett.

### BRACKEN'S WORLD

1. They worked for Century Studios, a movie company.
2. Leslie Neilsen was the second John Bracken (1970–1971). Warren Stevens (1969–70) was the first, but his role was different, because he was never seen on screen. Only Stevens's voice was used.

### CORONET BLUE

Michael Alden was played by Frank Converse, and he was in search of his true identity. He had recently suffered amnesia.

### EIGHT IS ENOUGH

1. The kids were (oldest to youngest) David, Mary, Joanie, Susan, Nancy, Elizabeth, Tommy, and Nicholas.
2. Bradford wrote for the *Sacramento Register*.
3. Tom's wife was Diana Hyland, who passed away early in the series.
4. Abby (Betty Buckley) taught at Memorial High.

### EMERGENCY

1. The series told the stories of Squad 51 of the Los Angeles County Fire Department's Paramedical Rescue Service.
2. Gage was played by Randolph Mantooth, and DeSoto by Kevin Tighe.
3. The series was called "Emergency + 4."

### FAMILY

1. The Lawrence family lived in Pasadena, California.
2. "Buddy" Lawrence was really Letitia Lawrence.

3. Doug was played by James Broderick. He was a lawyer.

## THE FAMILY HOLVAK

1. Tom Holvak was played by veteran Glenn Ford. He was a preacher. In fact, he was Reverend Tom Holvak.
2. Elizabeth Holvak was played by Julie Harris.

## HENNESEY

1. "Chick" Hennesey was played by Jackie Cooper.
2. Hennesey was stationed at a naval base in San Diego.
3. Nurse Hale was played by Abby Dalton.

## HERE COMES THE BRIDES

1. The Bolt brothers were Jason (Robert Brown), Jeremy (Bobby Sherman), and Joshua (David Soul).
2. The brides were brought to Seattle from New Bedford, Massachusetts.
3. Lottie Hatfield was played by Joan Blondell, and Captain Clancy by Henry Beckman.
4. The Bolts worked in a logging camp. Jason was the operator of the camp.

## KOLCHAK: THE NIGHT STALKER

1. Kolchak worked for the Chicago Independent News Service.
2. Vincenzo was played by Simon Oakland.

## THE LONG, HOT SUMMER

1. The series took place in the southern town of Frenchman's Bend.
2. The town was owned by "Boss" Will Varner. Varner was played by Edmund O'Brien (1965) and Dan O'Herlihy (1966).
3. Ben Quick, Varner's adversary, was played by Roy Thinnes.

## LUCAS TANNER

1. Tanner was played by David Hartman.
2. He taught at Harry S. Truman Memorial High School in Webster Groves, Missouri.
3. Glendon was played by Robbie Rist.

## MR. NOVAK

1. Novak was played by James Franciscus.
2. He taught at Jefferson High School in Los Angeles.
3. Woodridge was played by Burgess Meredith.

## THE PAPER CHASE

1. Houseman played Professor Charles W. Kingsfield, Jr.
2. Hart was played by James Stephens. He worked part-time at Ernie's pizza joint.
3. This series was filmed at Harvard.

## PEYTON PLACE

1. Peyton Place was a New England town.
2. Swain was the editor of *The Clarion*.
3. Farrow played Allison Mackenzie/Harrington.

## ROOM 222

1. This series took place in Walt Whitman High School.
2. Principal Seymour Kaufman was played by Michael Constantine.
3. Alice Johnson taught English.
4. Pete Dixon was played by Lloyd Haynes, and Liz McIntyre by Denise Nicholas.

## SAN FRANCISCO INTERNATIONAL AIRPORT

1. Jim Conrad was played by veteran Lloyd Bridges.
2. Bob Hatten was played by Clu Gulager.

## SARGE

1. Sarge (George Kennedy) was really Father Samuel Cavanaugh.
2. He was a priest at St. Aloysius Parish.
3. He had served nine years on the San Diego Police Department.

## SKAG

1. His name was Pete Skagska (Karl Malden), and he worked in a steel mill.
2. The series took place in Pittsburgh.
3. Jo Skagska was played by Piper Laurie.

## THE SMITH FAMILY

1. Smith was played by Henry Fonda.
2. Cindy (Darleen Carr) went to Los Angeles City College.
3. Bob Smith was played by Ron Howard.
4. The theme song was "Primrose Lane."

## THE WALTONS

1. The local paper was *The Blue Ridge Chronicle*.
2. Mary Ellen married Dr. Curtis Willard. He was killed at Pearl Harbor.
3. Maime was played by Helen Kleeb and Emily by Mary Jackson.

## THE WHITE SHADOW

1. Reeves (Ken Howard) coached at Carver High.
2. He had played for the Chicago Bulls.
3. Carver High won the Los Angeles City Basketball Championship.

## MATCHING (PAGES 95—96)

| | |
|---|---|
| 1. g | 7. l |
| 2. j | 8. d |
| 3. a | 9. f |
| 4. c | 10. i |
| 5. h | 11. k |
| 6. b | 12. e |

## THE FUGITIVE

1. Dr. Richard Kimble was played by David Janssen.
2. Diane Brewster played the role of Richard Kimble's wife, Helen.
3. William Conrad served as the show's narrator.
4. A train derailment enabled Richard Kimble to escape from Lieutenant Gerard.
5. Dr. Kimble's final words, moments before sentencing, were "For God, I'm innocent."
6. Kimble was found guilty of murder. The sentence was execution at the state penitentiary.
7. His search lasted for 4 years.
8. The final episode was titled "The Judgment" (Parts 1 and 2).
9. Helen Kimble was killed on September 19, 1961.
10. Lloyd Chandler, played by J. D. Cannon, was in the house the night Helen Kimble was murdered.
11. Jacqueline Scott played Richard Kimble's sister, Donna Taft.
12. Richard Kimble's brother-in-law was Leonard Taft, played by Richard Anderson.
13. Tuesday, September 5, was the day the running stopped.
Bonus: Richard Kimble lived with wife in Stafford, Indiana.

## STOP THE PRESSES!

### THE ANDROS TARGETS

1. Mike Andros was played by James Sutorius.
2. The series took place in New York.

### BIG TOWN

1. He was editor Steve Wilson.
2. Lorelei Kilbourne was played by five different actresses. Mary K. Wells (1950–51), Julie Stevens (1951–52), Jane Nigh (1952–53), Beverley Tyler (1953–54), and Trudy Wroe (1954–55) all played the revolving-door role.

### CRIME PHOTOGRAPHER

1. Casey was played by Richard Carlyle (1951) and Darren McGavin (1951–52).
2. Casey hung out at the popular Blue Note Cafe.
3. The Tony Mottola Trio provided musical interludes.

### THE FRONT PAGE

1. Burns was the paper's editor, Johnson his best reporter.
2. John Daly, who played Burns, was a news correspondent for CBS and ABC.

### FRONT PAGE DETECTIVE

1. David Chase was played by Edmund Lowe.
2. David's girl was played by Paula Drew. She was a fashion designer.

### I COVER TIMES SQUARE

1. Johnny Warren was played by Harold Huber.
2. He hung out at the out-of-town newsstand at Times Square.

### KINGSTON: CONFIDENTIAL

1. Kingston worked for the Frazier Group, located in San Francisco.
2. Frazier was played by Nancy Olson.

### LOU GRANT

1. The paper was owned by Margaret Pynchon (Nancy Marchand).
2. The managing editor was Charlie Hume (Mason Adams).

## NOT FOR PUBLICATION

Collins was played by William Adler and Jerome Cowan.

## THE REPORTER

1. Danny Taylor was played by Harry Guardino.
2. Artie Burns was a cabbie.

## THE ROARING TWENTIES

1. Scott Norris was played by Rex Reason, and Pat Garrison by Donald May.
2. Scott and Pat often went to the Charleston Club.
3. Pinky Pinkham, the singer, was played by perky Dorothy Provine.

## SAINTS AND SINNERS

Alexander was played by Nick Adams, and Lizzie by veteran Barbara Rush.

## TARGET: THE CORRUPTORS

Paul Marino (Stephen McNally) was the reporter, and Jack Flood (Robert Harland) was the undercover agent.

## WIRE SERVICE

1. Trans-Globe wire service was featured in this series.
2. The rerun title was "Deadline for Action."
3. Wells was played by Mercedes McCambridge.

## MATCHING (PAGE 102)

| | |
|---|---|
| 1. e | 5. h |
| 2. d | 6. c |
| 3. a | 7. b |
| 4. f | 8. i |
| | 9. g |

## MAKE 'EM LAUGH!

### THE ABBOTT & COSTELLO SHOW

1. The house was owned by Mr. Sidney Fields.
2. It was the Phoenix Coffee Shop.
3. Mike the Cop was played by Gordon Jones, Mr. Bacciagalupe by Joe Kirk, and Stinky by Joe Besser.

## THE ADVENTURES OF OZZIE & HARRIET

1. The series was produced and directed by Ozzie Nelson.
2. Dave worked part-time at Mr. Dobson's law office.

## AMOS 'N' ANDY

1. Amos was played by Alvin Childress, and Andy by Spencer Williams.
2. The series was set in Harlem.
3. Stevens was the head of the Mystics Knights of the Sea Lodge. He was called "The Kingfish."
4. Amos was a cabdriver.
5. Andy's girl friend was Madame Queen (Lillian Randolph).

## THE ANN SOTHERN SHOW

1. Katy was the assistant manager of the Bartley House hotel in New York.
2. Katy's best friend was Olive Smith, played by Ann Tyrrell.
3. Olive fell for dentist Delbart Gray (1960–61), as played by Louis Nye.

## BACHELOR FATHER

1. Bentley Gregg was an attorney.
2. Peter Tong was played by Samee Tong.
3. Peter's cousin's name was Charlie.
4. Linda Evans was once Linda Evensted.

## BLONDIE

1. Dagwood's boss was Mr. J. C. Dithers.
2. In the 1957 series, Dagwood was played by Arthur Lake, and Blondie by Pamela Britton.
3. In the 1968–69 series Dagwood was played by Will Hutchins, and Blondie was Patricia Harty.
4. Their dog's name was Daisey. The children were Alexander and Cookie.

## THE BOB CUMMINGS SHOW

1. This series was also aired as "Love That Bob."
2. Bob Collins was a professional photographer.
3. Margaret MacDonald was played by Rosemary DeCamp.

### THE DANNY THOMAS SHOW

1. The name of the series was "Make Room for Daddy" in its earliest seasons.
2. Danny was a nightclub entertainer at the Copa Club.
3. In 1970, the series ran as "Make Room for Grandaddy."
4. Charlie was played by Sid Melton, and Bunny was Pat Carroll.
5. Linda Williams was played by Angela Cartwright.

### DECEMBER BRIDE

1. Lily was played by Spring Byington.
2. Everyone was trying to find a husband for Lily.

### DENNIS THE MENACE

1. Dennis was created by cartoonist Hank Ketcham.
2. Dennis lived in Hillsdale.
3. Dennis's neighbor was Mr. Wilson. He was played by Joseph Kearns (1959–62) and Gale Gordon (1962–63).
4. Mr. Wilson collected rare coins.
5. Mr. Wilson's dog's name was Freemont.

### THE DONNA REED SHOW

1. Like Dennis, the Stones lived in Hillsdale.
2. Alex Stone was a doctor as played by Carl Betz.
3. "Johnny Angel" was introduced by Shelly Fabares (Mary Stone).

### FATHER KNOWS BEST

1. Jim was an agent for the General Insurance Company.
2. Kathy was "Kitten," Betty was "Princess," and James Junior was "Bud."
3. The Andersons lived in Springfield.
4. Margaret was played by Jane Wyatt.

### FIBBER McGEE AND MOLLY

1. The McGees lived at 79 Wistful Vista.
2. Fibber had a tendency to embellish the truth a bit. He also had a habit of overstuffing his hall closet and then having its contents erupt every time he opened it.

### THE GALE STORM SHOW

1. Susanna was the social director on the S.S. *Ocean Queen,* a luxury liner.
2. Susanna's best friend was Esmeralda Nugent, as played by Zazu Pitts.

## THE GEORGE BURNS AND GRACIE ALLEN SHOW

1. The Burnses' neighbors were Blanche and Harry Morton.
2. Harry Morton was played by Hal March (1950–1951), John Brown (1951), Fred Clark (1951–1953), and Larry Keating (1953–1958).
3. The series was produced in New York.

## THE GOLDBERGS

1. The Goldbergs lived at 1030 East Tremont Avenue, Bronx, New York, Apt. 3B.
2. Jake Goldberg was played by Philip Loeb (1949–51), Harold J. Stone (1952), and Robert H. Harris (1953–54).

## THE GREAT GILDERSLEEVE

1. His full name was Throckmorton P. Gildersleeve, and he was played by Willard Waterman.
2. Gildersleeve was the water commissioner for the town of Summerfield.
3. Leroy was played by Ronald Keith, and Marjorie by Stephanie Griffin.

## I MARRIED JOAN

1. Joan was married to Judge Bradley Stevens.
2. Joan Stevens was played by Joan Davis.

## LEAVE IT TO BEAVER

1. The Cleavers lived in Mayfield.
2. Beaver's teachers were Miss Canfield and Miss Landers.
3. Their full names were Whitey Whitney and Larry Mondello.
4. Clarence "Lumpy" Rutherford was played by Frank Bank, and Eddie Haskell by Ken Osmond.

## THE LIFE OF RILEY

1. In the first series, the Rileys were played by Jackie Gleason and Rosemary DeCamp. In the second run it was William Bendix and Marjorie Reynolds.
2. Riley worked in an aircraft plant in California.
3. Riley's famous phrase was "What a revoltin' development this is!"

## LIFE WITH FATHER

1. This series was set in New York City.
2. "Father" was Clarence Day, Jr., as played by Leon Ames.

## MAMA

1. Daughter Katrin, leafing through a family album, would say, "I remember my brother Nels . . . and my sister Dagmar . . . and, of course, Papa. But most of all, I remember Mama."
2. "Papa," as played by Judson Laire, was a carpenter.
3. "Mama" was played by Peggy Wood.

## THE MANY LOVES OF DOBIE GILLIS

1. Dobie lived in Central City.
2. Dobie's parents were Herbert T. Gillis (Frank Faylen) and Winifred Gillis (Florida Friebus).
3. Dobie's beatnik pal was Maynard G. Krebs (Bob Denver). His heartthrob was Thalia Menninger (beautiful Tuesday Weld).

## MR. PEEPERS

1. Mr. Peepers taught at Jefferson High School.
2. His full name was Robinson Peepers.
3. Harvey Weskit taught history and was played by Tony Randall.

## MY FRIEND IRMA

1. Irma was a secretary.
2. Irma lived with Jane Stacy (Cathy Lewis) in a Manhattan boardinghouse owned by Mrs. O'Reilly.
3. Mrs. Rhinelander was played by Margaret Dumont.

## MY LITTLE MARGIE

1. Vernon Albright worked for an investment counseling firm of Honeywell and Todd.
2. Margie shared an apartment on Fifth Avenue with her father.
3. Margie's boyfriend was Freddie Wilson (Don Hayden).

## OUR MISS BROOKS

1. Miss Brooks taught at Madison High School.
2. She was after Mr. Boynton (Robert Rockwell), the handsome biology teacher.
3. She found a job at Mrs. Nestor's Private Elementary School.

## THE PEOPLE'S CHOICE

1. Cooper played Socrates "Sock" Miller, a newly elected member of city council.
2. Sock got a job selling homes in Barkerville.
3. Sock married Amanda "Mandy" Peoples, the Mayor's daughter, as played by Pat Breslin.

## THE PHIL SILVERS SHOW

1. The series took place at fictitious Fort Baxter, Kansas.
2. The original title of this series was "You'll Never Get Rich."
3. Bilko was in charge of the motor pool.

## THE REAL McCOYS

1. The McCoys, originally from West Virginia, moved to California.
2. The farmhand was Pepino Garcia, played by Tony Martinez.
3. The series ran in reruns simply as "The McCoys."
4. Luke was played by Richard Crenna, and Kate squeakily by Kathy Nolan.

## TOPPER

1. They were all ghosts who returned to their former home after they died in a skiing accident (avalanche) in Europe.
2. The house was now owned by Cosmo Topper, played by Leo G. Carroll.

## MATCHING (PAGE 113)

| | | |
|---|---|---|
| 1. j | 5. a | 9. g |
| 2. d | 6. c | 10. k |
| 3. f | 7. l | 11. e |
| 4. h | 8. b | 12. i |

## I LOVE LUCY

1. Lucy's maiden name was MacGillicuddy.
2. Ricky worked at the Tropicana Club.
3. She wanted to be in Ricky's nightclub show.
4. Fred Mertz was William Frawley, and Ethel Mertz was Vivian Vance.
5. The series was set in New York City.
6. The Ricardos moved to Connecticut.
7. Ricky's club was called the Ricky Ricardo Babaloo Club.
8. Little Ricky was played by Richard Keith.
9. Lucy did a commercial for Vita-Veeta-Vegamin.
10. Washington said, "Please let me sit down. This is making me sick."
11. Adamson and Daniel wrote "I Love Lucy," the series theme song.
12. The young boy who got that tremendous crush on Lucy was Arthur Morton, played by Richard Crenna.
13. Little Ricky played the drums on the show.

14. Because he ran right from the club, he was dressed as an African Tribesman, complete with ringed nose and spear.
15. Ricky sang, "We're having a Baby, My Baby and Me."

## THE HONEYMOONERS

1. Norton described his occupation as a subterranean engineer.
2. Overdubbed, as it was in that episode, it was Bensonhurst-07741.
3. Ralph and Mr. Marshall were to play at Silver Oaks.
4. Ralph worked for the Gotham Bus Company.
5. Ralph's landlord was Mr. Johnson.
6. Norton was hit by a manhole cover on Himrod Street.
7. Norton's pet dog was named LuLu. He lost him in the Tunnel of Love in Coney Island.
8. The host of "The $99,000 Answer," Herb Norris, was played by Jay Jackson.
9. The dance teacher's name was Carlos Sanchez. He taught the mambo.
10. The Hurricanes (Ralph's team) were to play the Bayonne Bunch.
11. "Rhythm on Ice" supposedly starred Kenny Baker, Jan Frazee, Jerry Colonna, Buddy Ebsen, and Frankie Darrow.
12. The Kramdens' address was given as 328 Chauncey Street and 728 Chauncey Street.
13. Ralph's story was purchased by *American Weekly*.
14. Norton says there's trouble with the armature spacecraft interfering with the flow in the dyna-flow.
15. Ralph fishes at Fred's Landing.
16. Uncle Leo was married to Aunt Sarah. They lived in Utica.
17. Norton said, "Va-va-voom" when he found a copy of *Esquire*.
18. "Fortune" was left to Ralph by Mary Monahan.
19. Raccoon National Cemetery is in Bismark, North Dakota.
20. Andre of Morgan's Department Store offers to redecorate the Kramdens' apartment.
21. Ralph's bill broke the record low of .39¢ set by the Collier brothers.
22. Norton replaced Joe Hannigan in the play.
23. The boys are on their way to Norfolk, Virginia.
24. Norton lands a job with the Spiffy Iron Company.
25. They both make $62 a week.
26. Norton played handball against the butcher shop wall.
27. Alice was born February 8; Trixie on November 30.
28. Ralph is a Taurus, and Norton a Pisces.
29. They dined at the Colonade Room.
30. "Claves for Mambo" was recorded by Tito Rodriguez.
31. The Grand High Exalted Mystic Ruler was Morris Fink. He had three tails on his raccoon hat, while all the others had one.

32. August Gunther was the "Donut King."
33. Norton supposedly attended Oxford, in England.
34. Alice's sister was Agnes, and she married Stanley Saxon.
35. Captain Video was taking off for Pluto.
36. Norton bought a ring for his boss, Jim McKeever.
37. Ralph won the horse with the clock in its stomach at Salvatore's Pizzaria.
38. There was no room number. The door simply read Bureau of Internal Revenue—Tax Division.
39. The only officer of the Gotham Bus Co. to appear on the series was Mr. Douglas.
40. Uncle Leo gave Ralph and Alice a $25 gift certificate.

## KEEP 'EM LAUGHING!

### THE ADDAMS FAMILY

1. Lurch played the harpsichord.
2. Wednesday's middle name was Thursday.
3. Grandmama was played by Blossom Rock, and Cousin Itt by Felix Silla.
4. Gomez carried a lit cigar in his jacket pocket.

### THE ANDY GRIFFITH SHOW

1. Aunt Bea's best friend was Clara Edwards, as played by Hope Summers.
2. Barney's poem went as follows: "Juanite, Juanite, you are so sweet, from your head down to your feet."
3. Andy's first heartthrob was Ellie Walker, as played by Elinor Donahue.
4. The series was called "Andy of Mayberry" in syndication.
5. Floyd was played by Howard McNear.
6. Emmett owned and ran a fix-it shop.

### BEWITCHED

1. Samantha's father was Maurice, played by Maurice Evans.
2. Darrin worked for McMann and Tate, an advertising agency.
3. The Stephens' neighbors were Abner and Gladys Kravitz. Abner was played by George Tobias, Gladys by Alice Pearce and Sandra Gould.
4. Tabitha was played by Erin and Diane Murphy, identical twins.

### THE BILL COSBY SHOW

1. Cosby played Chet Kincaid, a high school physical education teacher.

2. Rose Kincaid was played by Lillian Randolph (1969–70) and Beah Richards (1970–71).
3. Marsha Peterson was played by Joyce Bulifant.

## THE BILL DANA SHOW

1. Dana played Jose Jimenez.
2. Jimenez worked as a bellhop at the Park Central Hotel.
3. Glick was played by Don Adams.

## THE BING CROSBY SHOW

1. Bing Crosby played Bing Collins. Ridiculous, heh?
2. He was a former singer who became an electrical engineer. Ridiculous, heh?
3. Ellie was played by Beverly Garland.

## THE BRADY BUNCH

1. The Bunch lived in a suburb of Los Angeles.
2. Mike Brady was an architect.
3. The kids were named Marcia, Jan, Cindy, Greg, Peter and Bobby.

## CAPTAIN NICE

1. William Daniels played Carter Nash, who was Captain Nice.
2. Nash was a chemist for the police department.
3. Captain Nice resided in Bigtown.
4. Mrs. Nash was played by Alice Ghostley.

## CAR 54, WHERE ARE YOU?

1. They worked in the 53rd precinct in the Bronx, New York.
2. Lucille Toody was played by Bea Pons.
3. Al Lewis, who would later play Grandpa on "The Munsters," played the role of officer Leo Schnauser.
4. Toody often said, "Ooo, Ooo, Ooo!"

## THE COURTSHIP OF EDDIE'S FATHER

1. Mrs. Livingston was played by Miyoshi Umeki.
2. Tom Corbett was a magazine publisher, played by Bill Bixby.
4. Norman Tinker was played by James Komack.

## THE DEBBIE REYNOLDS SHOW

Jim was a sports columnist for the Los Angeles Sun.

## THE DORIS DAY SHOW

1. Doris worked for *Today's World Magazine*. Her boss was Michael Nicholson (McLean Stevenson).
2. Doris's new boss was Cy Bennet (John Dehner).
3. Doris lived above Palucci's Italian Restaurant.

## F TROOP

1. Roaring Chicken was played by Edward Everett Horton, Bald Eagle by Don Rickles, Flaming Arrow by Phil Harris, and Milton Berle was Wise Owl.
2. Wrangler Jane was played by Melody Patterson.
3. The series was set at Fort Courage.
4. O'Rourke and Agarn were in association with the Hekawis, whose chief was Wild Eagle (Frank deKova).

## FAMILY AFFAIR

1. Bill Davis was a consulting engineer. He was played by Brian Keith.
2. His nephew was Jody, his nieces Buffy and Cissy.
3. Buffy's doll was Mrs. Beasley.
4. Giles French was called into service by the Queen of England. He was replaced by his brother Niles French.

## THE FARMER'S DAUGHTER

1. "Katy" was played by Inger Stevens.
2. Windom played Congressman Glen Morley.
3. Morley had two sons, Steve and Danny.
4. Agatha got up and down the stairs by way of an elevator seat.

## THE FLYING NUN

1. Sister Bertrille's former name was Elsie Ethington.
2. She served at Convent San Tanco near San Juan, Puerto Rico.
3. The Mother Superior was played by Madeleine Sherwood.

## GET SMART

1. K.A.O.S. was headed by Conrad Siegfried (Bernie Kopell). His right-hand man was Starker (King Moody).
2. The series was created by Mel Brooks and Buck Henry.
3. Hymie was played by Dick Gautier.
4. Agent Larrabee had the tendency of hiding in the oddest places.

## THE GHOST AND MRS. MUIR

1. The ghost was Captain Daniel Gregg, as played by Edward Mulhere.
2. The ghost's nephew was Claymore Gregg, as played by Charles Nelson Reilly.
3. The series was set in New England.

## GIDGET

1. Gidget was Francine Lawrence.
2. Gidget's best friend was Larue, as played by Lynette Winter.
3. Gidget's dad was Professor Russ Lawrence.

## GILLIGAN'S ISLAND

1. The boat was the S.S. *Minnow*.
2. Phil Silvers appeared as producer Harold Hekubaugh. The cast performed a musical version of *Hamlet*.
3. Maryann was from Kansas.

## GOMER PYLE, U.S.M.C.

1. Gomer was stationed at Camp Henderson, California.
2. Carter's girl friend was Bunny Harper, as played by Barbara Stuart.
3. Ronnie Schell played the role of Duke Slater.

## THE GOOD GUYS

1. The two lead characters were Bert Gramus (Herb Edelman) and Rufus Butterworth (Bob Denver).
2. The diner was called Bert's Place.
3. Big Tom was played by Alan Hale, Jr., who was reunited with Bob Denver. Hale played the Skipper on "Gilligan's Island".

## GOOD MORNING, WORLD

1. The station was owned by Roland B. Hutton, Jr. (Billy De Wolfe).
2. Sandy was played by Goldie Hawn.

## THE GOVENOR AND J.J.

1. "J.J." was Jennifer Jo was Julie Sommars.
2. J.J. took in a basset hound. She named it Guv.
3. Dancer-actor Dailey played Governor William Drinkwater.

## GREEN ACRES

1. The general store was owned by Sam Drucker (Frank Cady).
2. The carpenters were Alf and Ralph Monroe (Sid Melton and Mary Grace Canfield).
3. The pig's owners were Fred (Hank Patterson) and Doris Ziffel (Barbara Pepper and Fran Ryan).

## HAZEL

1. Hazel worked for the Baxters and the Johnsons.
2. George Baxter was a lawyer, played by Don DeFore.
3. Dorothy was played by Whitney Blake, and Harold by Bobby Buntrock.

## HE & SHE

1. Dick Hollister was played by Richard Benjamin. He created Jet-man.
2. Jetman was played by Oscar North, who was played by Jack Cassidy.
3. Paula was Paula Prentiss, and she was a social worker.

## HEY LANDLORD

1. The landlord was Woody Banner (Will Hutchins).
2. Woody inherited his building from his uncle.
3. Woody shared his apartment with Chuck Hookstratten (Sandy Baron).

## HOGAN'S HEROES

1. The series took place at Stalag 13.
2. From 1969–1970 Corporal Kinchloe was played by Kenneth Washington.
3. The colonel's secretaries were Helga (1965–66) and Hilda (1966–70).

## I DREAM OF JEANNIE

1. When Tony Nelson found her, Jeannie was 2,000 years old.
2. Nelson lived in Cocoa Beach, Florida.
3. Yes! Tony and Jeannie were married in 1969.

## I'M DICKENS—HE'S FENSTER

Arch Fenster was played by Marty Ingels, and Harry Dickens by John Astin. They were both carpenters.

## IT'S ABOUT TIME

1. The astronauts were Hector and Mac, played by Jack Mullaney and Frank Aletter.
2. The quartet that played the cave family were named Shad (mom), Gronk (dad), Mlor (daughter), and Breer (son).

## THE JOEY BISHOP SHOW

1. Joey Bishop was Joey Barnes, an assistant to a Los Angeles press agent.
2. Madge Blake was Joey's wife from 1961 to 1962, and from 1962 to 1965 the role was played by Abby Dalton.

## JULIA

1. Julia worked in the medical office at Astrospace Industries.
2. Corey Baker was played by Marc Coppage.
3. Her neighbor's were the Waggedorns (Marie, Len, and son Earl J.) Len was a police officer.

## THE LUCY SHOW

1. Originally, Lucy lived in Danfield, Connecticut, then San Francisco (1965), and then she relocated to Los Angeles (1968).
2. Lucy first worked at Danfield First National Bank, then Westland Bank (San Francisco), and then at the Carter Employment Agency in Los Angeles.
3. The show was called "Here's Lucy" in 1968.

## MAYBERRY R.F.D.

1. Sam Jones was played by Ken Berry.
2. Sam's girl friend was Millie Swanson, as played by Arlene Golonka.
3. Aunt Alice was played by Alice Ghostley.

## McHALE'S NAVY

1. The men called him "Old Lead Bottom."
2. The show relocated in Voltafiore, Italy.

## MICKEY

1. Mickey inherited the Marina Palms in Newport Harbor, California.
2. The loan was held by Ling Savings & Loan, owned by relatives of hotel manager Sammy Ling (Samee Tong).
3. Timmy Grady was played by Tim Rooney, Mickey's real-life son.

## MR. TERRIFIC

1. Mr. Terrific was really Stanley Beamish, who was played by Stephen Strimpell. He owned a gas station.
2. The secret pills were developed by the Bureau of Secret Projects, whose chief was Barton J. Reed (John McGiver).
3. The pills only worked on one man, Stanley Beamish.

## THE MONKEES

The Monkees were Davey Jones, Peter Tork, Mike Nesmith, and Micky Dolenz.

## THE MOTHERS-IN-LAW

1. Roger Buell was played by Roger Carmel (1967–68) and Richard Deacon (1968–69).
2. Roger was a television writer and Herb a lawyer.
3. Eve Hubbard was once a champion golfer.

## THE MUNSTERS

1. The Munsters lived at 1313 Mockingbird Lane.
2. Herman worked for the funeral home of Gateman, Goodbury, and Graves.
3. Eddie had a werewolf doll.
4. Herman was 150 years old.

## MY FAVORITE MARTIAN

1. Uncle Martin was played by Ray Walston, and Tim O'Hara by Bill Bixby.
2. Tim worked for *The Los Angeles Sun*. He was a reporter.
3. Their next-door neighbor was Lorelei Brown, played by Pamela Britton. She was famous for her brownies.

## MY LIVING DOLL

1. Rhoda was a robot—A709, to be specific.
2. Cummings played a psychiatrist, Dr. Robert McDonald.

## MY MOTHER THE CAR

1. The voice of the car was Ann Sothern. The car was a 1928 Porter.
2. Mancini was played by Avery Schrieber.
3. Dave's kids were Cindy and Randy.

## MY THREE SONS

1. "Bub" O'Casey was played by William Frawley.
2. Mike was played by Tim Considine. He left home after getting married, to accept a college teaching job.
3. The family moved to North Hollywood, California.
4. The triplets were named Steven, Charlie, and Robbie. They were played by Joseph, Michael, and Daniel Todd.

## MY WORLD AND WELCOME TO IT

1. William Windom played writer-cartoonist John Monroe.
2. Ellen was played by Joan Hotchkiss, and Lydia by Lisa Gerritsen.
3. The series was based on the works of James Thurber.

## NO TIME FOR SERGEANTS

1. Airman Will Stockdale was played by Sammy Jackson.
2. Jackson was stationed at Oliver Air Force Base.

## THE PATTY DUKE SHOW

1. Patty's brother was Ross Lane, as played by Paul O'Keefe.
2. The Lane family lived in Brooklyn Heights, New York.
3. Patty's boyfriend, Richard, was a part-time Western Union messenger.

## PETTICOAT JUNCTION

1. Billie Jo was played by Jeannine Riley (1963–65), Gunilla Hutton (1965–66), and Meredith MacRae (1966–70). Bobbie Jo was played by Pat Woodell (1963–65) and Lori Saunders (1965–70). Betty Jo was played by Linda Kaye Henning.
2. The Shady Rest Hotel was in Hooterville.
3. Kate Bradley was played by Bea Benaderet, and Uncle Joe Carson by Edgar Buchanan.

## PLEASE DON'T EAT THE DAISIES

1. Jim Nash was a professor of English at Ridgemont College.
2. The Nashes' neighbors were Marge and Herb Thornton.
3. Joan was a newspaper columnist.

## THE SECOND HUNDRED YEARS

1. Luke died in a freak glacier slide in Alaska.
2. Edwin Carpenter was played by Arthur O'Connell.
3. Edwin Carpenter lived in Woodland Oaks, California.

## TAMMY

1. Tammy Tarleton was played by Debbie Watson.
2. Grandpa Tarleton was played by Denver Pyle.
3. Tammy worked for plantation owner John Brent (Donald Woods).

## THAT GIRL

1. "That Girl" was Ann Marie, played by lovely Marlo Thomas.
2. Ann's beau was Donald Hollinger, an employee of *Newsview Magazine*. He was played by Ted Bessell.
3. They were never married on the program.
4. Ann's parents, Lou and Helen, lived in Brewster, New York.

## TO ROME WITH LOVE

1. Endicott was a college professor, played by John Forsythe.
2. Endicott moved from Iowa to accept a teaching job at the American Overseas School.
3. Endicott's daughters were Penny and Alison.

## MATCHING (PAGE 132)

| | | |
|---|---|---|
| 1. g | 6. f | 11. m |
| 2. k | 7. b | 12. n |
| 3. d | 8. h | 13. j |
| 4. i | 9. o | 14. c |
| 5. a | 10. e | 15. l |

## THE BEVERLY HILLBILLIES

1. Granny's name was Daisy Moses, as played by Irene Ryan.
2. Milburn Drysdale was played by Raymond Bailey, Margaret Drysdale by Harriet MacGibbon, and Sonny Drysdale by Louis Nye.
3. The show's theme was sung by Lester Flatt and Earl Scruggs.
4. Elly fell for Hollywood actor Dash Riprock (1965–1969).
5. Elly described the new built-in pool as the "cement pond."
6. The Clampetts lived in Bugtussle, Tennessee.
7. Drysdale worked at the Commerce Bank. His secretary, Jane Hathaway, was played by Nancy Kulp.
8. Mrs. Drysdale's poodle was named Claude.
9. Pearl Bodine was played by Bea Benaderet.
10. The Clampetts purchased the Mammoth Studios.

## THE DICK VAN DYKE SHOW

1. Rob wrote for the "Alan Brady Show."
2. Rob's co-writers were Sally Rodgers (Rose Marie) and Buddy Sorrell (Morey Amsterdam).
3. Richie's middle name was Rosebud.
4. Jerry Helper was a dentist.
5. Richard Deacon played Mel Cooley, Alan Brady's brother-in-law and flunky.
6. The Petries lived in New Rochelle, New York.
7. Stanley was a duck.
8. When connected, Rob's freckles formed the liberty bell, crack and all.
9. Laura was a dancer before she married Rob.
10. The couple were the Petersons, and they were black.


## THEY'RE STILL LAUGHING!

### ALL IN THE FAMILY

1. The Bunkers lived at 704 Hauser Street, Queens, New York.
2. Archie was a foreman for the Prendergast Tool and Die Company. He moonlighted as a cab driver.
3. Both "The Jeffersons" and "Maude" were spin-offs from "All in the Family."
4. Edith's maiden name was Baines.

### ALL'S FAIR

1. Richard Barrington was played by Richard Crenna and Charlotte Drake by Bernadette Peters.
2. Barrington was a political columnist and Drake a reporter for CBS News.
3. The series took place in Washington, D.C.

### ARNIE

1. Arnie Nuvo was played by Hershel Bernardi.
2. Lillian Nuvo was played by Sue Ann Langdon.
3. Arnie's boss was Hamilton Majors, Jr. (Roger Bowen). He worked at the Continental Flange Company.

### THE BAD NEWS BEARS

1. Buttermaker, played by Jack Warden, coached the Hoover Junior High baseball team.
2. Buttermaker was formerly a swimming-pool cleaner.
3. Buttermaker's female pitcher was Amanda Whirlitzer.

## BALL FOUR

1. The series revolved around the Washington Americans.
2. Manager "Cap" Capagrossa was played by James Somack.
3. Jim Bouton played Jim Barton.

## BAREFOOT IN THE PARK

1. The series took place in New York.
2. Paul was played by Scoey Mitchell, his wife, Corie, by Tracy Reed.

## BARNEY MILLER

1. The 12th Precinct was in Greenwich Village.
2. Barney's two kids were named David and Rachael.
3. Harris's book was titled "Blood on the Badge."

## BLANSKY'S BEAUTIES

1. Nancy Blansky was played by Nancy Walker.
2. Nancy worked at the Oasis Hotel.
3. Bambi was played by Caren Kaye.

## BOB & CAROL & TED & ALICE

1. Bob was Robert Urich, Carol was Anne Archer, Ted was David Spielberg, and Alice was Anita Gillette.
2. Bob was a filmmaker, and Ted was a lawyer.

## THE BOB CRANE SHOW

1. Bob Wilcox was an executive at an insurance company.
2. He quit to attend medical school.
3. Ernest Bosso, Bob's landlord, was played by Ronny Graham.

## THE BOB NEWHART SHOW

1. The series was set in Chicago.
2. Florida Friebus, Dobie Gillis's mother, played Mrs. Bakerman.
3. Howard's brother was Gordon Borden, and he was a warden.

## THE BRIAN KEITH SHOW

1. Keith played Dr. Sean Jamison.
2. Dr. Anne Jamison was played by Shelley Fabares.
3. The series took place in Oahu, Hawaii.

## BRIDGET LOVES BERNIE

1. Bridget was played by Meredith Baxter, and Bernie by David Birney. They later married in real life.
2. Bridget was an elementary school teacher.
3. Bernie drove a cab to make ends meet.

## C.P.O. SHARKEY

1. Sharkey was stationed at the Navy Training Center in San Diego, California.
2. The base commander was lovely Elizabeth Allen, who played Captain Quinlan.

## CALUCCI'S DEPARTMENT

1. Joe Calucci was played by James Coco.
2. Joe worked at the New York State Unemployment Office.
3. Candy Azzara played Shirley Balukis.

## CARTER COUNTRY

1. The series took place in Clinton Corners, Georgia.
2. Carter was then-President Carter.
3. Mobey was played by Victor French.

## THE CHICAGO TEDDY BEARS

1. Linc and his uncle owned a speakeasy.
2. Linc McCray was played by Dean Jones, and Uncle Latzi by John Banner.
3. Art Metrano, later to star in "Joanie Loves Chiachi," appeared as Nick Marr.

## CHICO AND THE MAN

1. The theme song, "Chico and the Man," was written and performed by Jose Feliciano.
2. His full name was Ed Brown, and he was played by Jack Albertson.
3. His aunt was Aunt Charo, played by Charo.

## THE CORNER BAR

1. The bar was called "Grant's Tomb."
2. Harry was played by Gabriel Dell, an original Bowery Boy.
3. Shimen Ruskin played Meyer Shapiro.
4. Fred Costello (J. J. Barry) was a cabbie, while Donald (Ron Carey) was an actor of some very small measure.

### DIANA

1. Diana worked at Butler's Department Store.
2. Holly Green, a model played by Carol Androsky, was Diana's friend and neighbor.

### DOC

1. "Doc" was played by Bernard Hughes.
2. The locale for "Doc" was New York City.
3. The clinic was run by Stanley Moss, as played by David Ogden Stiers.

### THE DON RICKLES SHOW

1. Don was an advertising executive for Kingston, Cohen and Vanderpool, Inc.
2. The Robinsons lived on Long Island, New York.
3. Barbara Robinson was played by Louise Sorel.

### FUNNY FACE

1. The lead role of Sandy Stockton was played by Sandy Duncan.
2. Sandy was a student at U.C.L.A.

### THE GOOD LIFE

1. Albert Miller was played by Larry Hagman, and Jane Miller by Donna Mills.
2. Albert became a butler and Jane a cook.
3. The couple worked as servants to Charles Dutton (Danny Goldman).

### GRANDPA GOES TO WASHINGTON

1. Senator Kelley (Jack Albertson) was elected when the other candidates were found to be crooks.
2. His son was Major General Kevin Kelley, as played by Larry Linville.
3. Joe drove a Volkswagen.

### HAPPY DAYS

1. Richie attended Jefferson High in Milwaukee, Wisconsin.
2. A "Happy Days" episode was first seen as a segment of "Love American Style." Many of the actors were the same.
3. Of course, Arnold first owned Arnold's. He was played by Pat Morita. The second owner was Al Delvecchio, as played by Al Molinaro, of "Odd Couple" fame.
4. Richie and Ralph were stationed in Greenland.

## HOT L BALTIMORE

1. Hot L Baltimore was Hotel Baltimore without the "E," which is how the sign outside the hotel read.
2. Bill Lewis was played by James Cromwell.
3. The hotel manager was Clifford Ainsley, as played by Richard Masur.

## THE JIMMY STEWART SHOW

1. Howard taught at Josiah Kessel College.
2. He taught anthropology.
3. The Howards resided in Easy Valley, California.

## LOTSA LUCK

1. Dom DeLuise starred as Stanley Belmont, a New York City Bus Company employee.
2. Mrs. Belmont was played by Kathleen Freeman.
3. Stanley's sister was Olive (Beverly Sanders), and his brother-in-law was Arthur (Wynn Irwin).

## M*A*S*H

1. M*A*S*H is Mobile Army Surgical Hospital.
2. Blake's plane was shot down over the Sea of Japan.
3. Hot Lips married Lieutenant Colonel Donald Penobscott.
4. Radar was born in Iowa.

## MAUDE

1. The Findlays lived in Tuckahoe, New York.
2. Walter owned Findlay's Friendly Appliances.
3. The Findlays' neighbors were the Harmans. Arthur was played by Conrad Bain, and Vivian by Rue McClanahan.

## THE McLEAN STEVENSON SHOW

1. Ferguson lived in Evanston, Illinois.
2. Mac owned a hardware store.
3. Peggy was played by Barbara Stuart.

## MORK & MINDY

1. Mork landed near Boulder, Colorado.
2. The Orkan leader was named Orson.
3. Mindy's father was Frederick McConnell, as played by Conrad Janis. He ran a music store.

## THE NANCY WALKER SHOW

1. Nancy Walker played the role of Nancy Kitteridge.
2. Nancy ran the Nancy Kitteridge Talent Agency.
3. Nancy resided in Hollywood.
4. Nancy's husband, Lieutenant Commander Kenneth Kitteridge, played by William Daniels, would spend only two months a year with his wife, when he had shore leave.

## NANNY AND THE PROFESSOR

1. Phoebe replaced Miss Dunbar as nanny to the Everett kids.
2. Professor Everett was played by Richard Long.
3. The Everett children were Hal, Butch, and Prudence.

## THE NEW ANDY GRIFFITH SHOW

1. Andy Griffith played the role of Andy Sawyer.
2. Andy returned to Greenwood to finish a mayoral term left vacated by the retiring mayor.
3. Lee Sawyer was played by Lee Meriweather.

## THE NEW DICK VAN DYKE SHOW

1. The Prestons lived in Phoenix, Arizona.
2. Jenny Preston was played by Hope Lange.
3. The Prestons moved to Hollywood so that Dick could accept an acting job in the soap opera "Those Who Care."

## ON THE ROCKS

1. The prison used as the setting was Alamesa Minimum Security Prison.
2. Fuentes was played by Jose Perez and Cleaver by Rick Hurst.

## OPERATION PETTICOAT

1. Lieutenant Commander Matthew Sherman was played by John Astin.
2. His submarine was the *Sea Tiger*. It was pink.

## PAPER MOON

1. The show took place throughout Kansas.
2. Moses Pray was played by Christopher Connelly, and Addie Pray by Jodie Foster.

## THE PARTRIDGE FAMILY

1. The Partridge family rode around in a multi-colored bus.
2. The band's agent was Reuben Kinkaid, as played by Dave Madden.
3. The Partridge kids were Keith (David Cassidy), Lauri (Susan Dey), Danny (Danny Bonaduce), Christopher (Jeremy Gelbwaks and Brian Foster), and Tracy (Suzanne Crough).

## THE PAUL LYNDE SHOW

1. The Simms lived in Ocean Grove, California.
2. Howie had a genius I. Q.
3. Howie's parents were played by the comedy team of Jerry Stiller and Anne Meara.

## PAUL SAND IN FRIENDS AND LOVERS

1. Dreyfuss was a bass violinist for the Boston Symphony.
2. Ben Dreyfuss was played by Jack Gilford.
3. Fred Meyerbach was played by Steve Landesberg.

## PHYLLIS

1. Phyllis moved to San Francisco to live with Lars's mother.
2. Phyllis worked at Erskine's Commercial Photography Studio.
3. "Mother Dexter" was played by Judith Lowry.

## POPI

1. The series was based on the movie *Popi*.
2. "Popi" was played by Hector Elizondo. He lived in New York City.
3. The Rodriquez boys were named Junior and Luis.

## RHODA

1. Rhoda married Joe Gerard, the owner of the New York Wrecking Company.
2. Rhoda found a job at the Doyle Costume Company.
3. Brenda was played by Julie Kavner. Her boyfriend, Benny Goodwin, was played by Ray Buktenica.

## SANFORD AND SON

1. Esther's husband's name was Woody.
2. Donna Harris was played by Lynn Hamilton.
3. Whitman Mayo played Grady Wilson, and Don Bexley played Bubba Hoover.

## STOCKARD CHANNING IN JUST FRIENDS

1. Susan Hughes worked at the Fountain of Youth.
2. Susan moved from Boston to Los Angeles.

## TABITHA

1. Tabitha was played by lovely Lisa Hartman.
2. Tabitha worked for television station KLXA in Los Angeles.
3. Aunt Minerva was played by Karen Morrow.

## TEMPERATURES RISING

1. Capital General Hospital was the setting for this series.
2. Dr. Noland was played by Cleavon Little and Dr. Mercy by Paul Lynde.

## THE TONY RANDALL SHOW

1. Randall played Judge Walter Franklin.
2. Roberta or "Bobby" Franklin was played by Devon Scott (1976–77) and Penny Peyser (1977–78).
3. Wyatt Franklin, Walter's dad, was played by Hans Conried.

## THE WAVERLY WONDERS

1. Joe Casey was also a history teacher at Waverly High.
2. Joe Casey was played by Joe Namath.
3. Waverly High was in Eastfield, Wisconsin.

## WELCOME BACK KOTTER

1. The school that served as this show's setting was James Buchanan High School.
2. The twins' names were Rachel and Robin.
3. White played Mr. Michael Woodman, the school's assistant principal and then principal.

## WHEN THINGS WERE ROTTEN

1. Robin was played by Dick Gautier.
2. Friar Tuck was played by Dick Van Patten and Alan-a-Dale by Bernie Kopell.
3. The series was created by Mel Brooks.

## MATCHING (PAGES 149–150)

1. i
2. d
3. l
4. a
5. g
6. b

| | | |
|---|---|---|
| 7. n | 10. m | 13. j |
| 8. k | 11. f | 14. e |
| 9. c | 12. h | 15. o |

## THE MARY TYLER MOORE SHOW

1. The series was set in Minneapolis.
2. Mary worked at WJM-TV. Her boss was Lou Grant (Ed Asner).
3. Murray Slaughter was the head writer, as played by Gavin MacLeod.
4. Georgette's maiden name was Franklin.
5. Ted and Georgette adopted a boy named David.
6. Sue Ann starred in "The Happy Homemaker Show."
7. Lou Grant's wife's name was Edie, as played by Priscilla Morrill.
8. The theme song for this series was "Love Is All Around."
9. Ted always began his life story with "It all started in a five-thousand-watt radio station in Fresno, California."
10. Gordie was played by John Amos. Ted called him "Gord-o."

## THE ODD COUPLE

1. Oscar's bookie was "52nd Street Irwin."
2. Felix's doctor was Dr. Melnitz. Oscar was operated on by Dr. Krakower.
3. The boys went to Hoklahoma on vacation.
4. Felix and Gloria went to Santo Domingo on their honeymoon.
5. Felix "scalped" tickets to "Kiss My Face."
6. Oscar won Golden Earrings from Salty and raced him in Miami.
7. Felix's business was F.U. Enterprises.
8. The boys went to Burger's Fat Farm.
9. Felix's parrot's name was Albert.
10. Felix named the dog Yawbus. (That's "Subway" backwards.)
11. The boys dressed as a horse. (Oscar brought up the rear.)
12. Mrs. Madison would consume chocolate when she was upset.
13. Both Marilyn Horne and Richard Fredericks appeared on the show.
14. Felix wanted to buy plot #204 by the babbling brook.
15. John Astin played the head of the playboy magazine.
16. Edna was originally played by Pamela Ferdin.
17. The guard dog at the security apartment was "Peaches."
18. Oscar posed in ads for Mandar cologne.
19. Coach Unger suggested a play called "The Disjointed U."
20. The name of Felix's poem was "Ode to a Skyscraper."

## TELEVISION'S BEST FRIEND

### THE ADVENTURES OF CHAMPION

1. Champion was owned by Ricky North, played by Barry Curtis.
2. The ranch was owned by Ricky's Uncle Sandy.
3. Champion only allowed Ricky to ride him.

### THE ADVENTURES OF RIN TIN TIN

1. Rin Tin Tin was owned by Rusty, played by Lee Aaker.
2. The soldiers were stationed at Fort Apache, Arizona.
3. Rin Tin Tin's trainer was Les Duncan.

### FLIPPER

1. Flipper was played by a dolphin named Suzy.
2. Porter Ricks was played by Brian Kelly. He was chief ranger of Coral Key Park in Florida.
3. There were two children: Sandy, age 15, and Bud, age 10.

### GENTLE BEN

1. Tom Wedloe was played by Dennis Weaver.
2. Mark was played by Clint Howard.
3. Ben was an American black bear, who weighed in at over 600 pounds.
4. The Wedloes lived in the Florida Everglades.

### LASSIE

1. Lassie's first owner was Jeff Miller (1954–1957). He was played by Tommy Rettig.
2. The Millers and Lassie lived in Calverton.
3. Tom Provost played the role of the orphan runaway Timmy, who was taken in by the Millers.
4. Ruth was first played by Cloris Leachman (1957–1958) and then by June Lockhart (1958–1964).

### MR. ED

1. Wilbur Post was played by Alan Young.
2. The voice of Mr. Ed was Allan "Rocky" Post.
3. Wilbur made his living as an architect.

## MY FRIEND FLICKA

1. Flicka was a horse.
2. Flicka was owned by the McLaughlins and young Ken in particular. He was played by Johnny Washbrook.
3. The series's locale was Montana.

## FIND MY OWNER

1. Muffit was the mechanical canine on "Battlestar Galactica" (1978–80, ABC).
2. Stormy was the St. Bernard, and Bandie the Pekingese on "Life with Elizabeth" (1953–55; syndicated).
3. Silver and Scout were the horses from "The Lone Ranger" (1949–57, ABC).
4. Buttons was the chimp on "Me & the Chimp" (1972, CBS).
5. Spot was the dragon and Igor was the bat on "The Munsters" (1964–66, CBS).
6. Kitty was the lion on "The Addams Family" (1964–66, ABC).
7. Tramp was the dog on "My Three Sons" (1960–72, ABC and CBS).
8. Waldo was the sheepdog and Myrtle was the pig on "Nanny and the Professor" (1970–71, ABC).
9. Ladadog was the sheepdog on "Please Don't Eat the Daisies" (1965–67, CBS).
10. Oregano was the pooch on "Shirley" (1979–80, ABC).
11. Neil was the St. Bernard on "Topper" (1953–56, CBS, NBC, and ABC).
12. Tornado and Phantom were stallions (one white, one black) on "Zorro" (1957–59, ABC).
13. Bingo was the chimp on "The Abbott and Costello Show" (1951–53; syndicated).
14. Jasper was the shaggy dog on "Bachelor Father" (1957–62, CBS, NBC, and ABC).
15. Fred was the cockatoo on "Baretta" (1975–78, ABC).
16. Max was the bionic dog on "The Bionic Woman" (1976–78, ABC and NBC).
17. Tiger was the shaggy dog on "The Brady Bunch" (1969–74, ABC).
18. Arnold was the pig on "Green Acres" (1965–71, CBS).
19. Bimbo was the elephant on "Circus Boy" (1956–58, NBC and ABC).
20. Clarence was the lion, and Judy the chimp on "Daktari" (1966–69, CBS).
21. Scruffy was the dog on "The Ghost and Mrs. Muir" (1968–70, NBC and ABC).

22. Charlie, Enoch, and Cindy were chimps on "The Hathaways" (1961–62, ABC).
23. Gin-Gin was the pooch on "I Dream of Jeannie" (1965–70, NBC).
24. King was the horse on "National Velvet" (1960–62, NBC).
25. Chipper was the dog on "Land of the Giants" (1968–70, ABC).
26. Simone was the dog on "The Partridge Family" (1970–74, ABC).
27. Muffin was the dog on "The Ropers" (1979–80, ABC).
28. Trigger and Buttermilk were horses and Bullet was the dog on "The Roy Rogers Show" (1951–57, NBC).
29. Yukon King was the dog, and Rex was the horse, on "Sergeant Preston of the Yukon" (1955–58, CBS).
30. Cheetah was the chimp on "Tarzan" (1966–69, NBC and CBS).
31. Cleo was the dog on "People's Choice" (1955–58, ABC).
32. Bruce was the ocelot on "Honey West" (1965–66, ABC).
33. Snow was the dog on "The Monroes" (1966–67, ABC).
34. Lord Nelson was the sheepdog on "The Doris Day Show" (1968–73, CBS).
35. Ginger and LuLu were dogs featured on specific episodes of "The Honeymooners" (1955–56, CBS).

## TELEVISION GRAB BAG

### TITLE MATCHING (PAGE 158)

| | | |
|---|---|---|
| 1. f | 5. a | 9. b |
| 2. c | 6. g | 10. l |
| 3. h | 7. d | 11. e |
| 4. k | 8. i | 12. j |

### CRIME DRAMA MATCHING (PAGES 158–159 )

| | | |
|---|---|---|
| 1. e | 5. f | 9. g |
| 2. h | 6. j | 10. i |
| 3. a | 7. c | 11. b |
| 4. l | 8. d | 12. k |

### SPINOFF MATCHING (PAGE 159)

| | | |
|---|---|---|
| 1. k | 5. g | 9. c |
| 2. h | 6. a | 10. e |
| 3. j | 7. l | 11. d |
| 4. i | 8. f | 12. b |

### YOUR HOST FOR THE EVENING...

1. "Alcoa Premiere" was hosted by Fred Astaire.
2. "Alcoa Presents" was hosted by John Newland.

3. "Cowboy Theater" was hosted by Monty Hall.
4. "Damon Runyon Theater" was hosted by Donald Woods.
5. "Favorite Story" was hosted by Adolphe Menjou.
6. "Frontier Justice" was hosted by Lew Ayres, Melvyn Douglas, and Ralph Bellamy.
7. "General Electric Theater" was hosted by Ronald Reagan.
8. "Ghost Story" was hosted by Sebastian Cabot.
9. "Omnibus" was hosted by Alistair Cooke.
10. "Schlitz Playhouse of Stars" was hosted by Irene Dunne.
11. "Silver Theater" was hosted by Conrad Nagel.
12. "Suspicion" was originally hosted by Dennis O'Keefe.
13. The two hosts of the "20th Century Fox Hour" were Joseph Cotten (1955–56) and Robert Sterling (1956–57).
14. "Warner Brothers Presents" was hosted by Gig Young.
15. "West Point Story" was hosted by Donald May, who played the role of Cadet Charles C. Thompson.

## NAME THAT TV THEME!

1. The theme from "Alfred Hitchcock Presents" was "Funeral March of the Marionette."
2. The theme from "The Courtship of Eddie's Father" was "Best Friends."
3. The theme from "Dr. Kildare" was "Three Stars Will Shine Tonight."
4. The theme from "The Donna Reed Show" was "Happy Days."
5. The theme from "Dragnet" was "Dragnet."
6. The theme from "The Gene Autry Show" was "Back in the Saddle Again."
7. The theme from "The Burns & Allen Show" was "Love Nest."
8. The theme from "The Greatest Show on Earth" was "March of the Clowns."
9. The theme from "Gunsmoke" was "Gunsmoke Trails."
10. The theme from "The Lone Ranger" was "The William Tell Overture."
11. The theme from "M*A*S*H" was "Suicide Is Painless."
12. The theme from "Medic" was "Blue Star."
13. The theme from "The Paper Chase" was "The First Years."
14. The theme from "The Partridge Family" was "Come On, Get Happy."
15. The theme from "The Roy Rogers Show" was "Happy Trails to You."

# TOTAL TV OBSCURITY!

OBSCURE POTPOURRI

1. Alan Young played himself on "The Alan Young Show."
2. The contest was run by *The Flushing Tribune*.
3. Annie Oakley was played by Gail Davis.
4. Gregg's phone number was CRestview 5–4699.
5. Dr. Cassandra was played by Ida Lupino.
6. The family doctor was Dr. Bombay (Bernard Fox).
7. The bus stop was in Sunrise, Colorado.
8. Dante was played by veteran Howard Duff.
9. Eve Arden starred in "The Eve Arden Show" (1957–58 on CBS).
10. Lisa Benton worked for Sunwest Airlines.
11. The host of "Gangbusters" was Phillips H. Lord, its creator.
12. Gibbsville was in Pennsylvania.
13. "The Skipper" was really Jonas Grumby.
14. Mr. Angel was played by comic genius Carl Reiner.
15. The theme from "The Green Hornet" was played by Al Hirt.
16. Hec Ramsey lived in New Prospect, Oklahoma.
17. "Seattle" was sung by The New Establishment.
18. James Arness starred in "How the West Was Won" (1978–79 on ABC).
19. Sylvia was played by Carol Lynley.
20. Kentucky Jones was played by Dennis Weaver.
21. Lassie's trainer was Rudd Weatherwax.
22. Elizabeth was played by Betty White.
23. Betty Ramsey was played by Mary Jane Croft.
24. Burnley worked at Krockmeyer's Department Store.
25. Beauregard was played by Roger Moore.
26. Colonel McCauley was played by William Ludigan.
27. Michael Anthony was played by Marvin Miller.
28. Captain Morton was played by Richard X. Slattery.
29. Moses was played by Burt Lancaster, and Aaron by Anthony Quayle.
30. MacMurray played Fergus McBain Douglas (1971–72), Steve's cousin.
31. Norby worked at the Pearl River First National Bank.
32. Brennan was played by George Hamilton.
33. Rodney Harrington was played by Ryan O'Neal.
34. Molly Gibbons was played by Dena Dietrich.
35. Barbara Billingsley, the future Mrs. Cleaver, played Mrs. Wilson.
36. Mrs. Pruitt was played by Phyllis Diller.

37. Ray Milland (as Professor Ray McNutley) taught at both Lynn-haven College and Cromstock University.
38. The riverboat was the *Enterprise*.
39. The houseboat was named *Our Boat*.
40. Sheena was played by Irish McCalla.
41. Slattery was played by Richard Crenna.
42. Dick Smothers worked for Pandora Publications.
43. Sugar was played by Barbi Benton, Marianne Black, and Didi Carr.
44. Tracy Carlyle Hastings was played by Lana Turner.
45. The escorts in "The Time Express" were Vincent Price and real-life wife Carol Browne.


## THE ADVENTURES OF OZZIE & HARRIET

1. Harriet was preparing tollhouse cookies on the premiere episode.
2. Nancy Baker called David about a school dance.
3. "Thorny's" wife's name was Kathryn. His son was Will.
4. According to the premiere, Thorny had gone steady with seven girls and Ozzie only one. Guess who?


## THE ANDY GRIFFITH SHOW

1. Sheriff Taylor's license plate number was JL327.
2. The choir performed song number 14A.
3. Ten pounds of potatoes sold for 29¢.


## BEVERLY HILLBILLIES

1. The oil company was located in Tulsa, Oklahoma.
2. Jed was offered between $25,000,000 and $100,000,000, depending on the amount of oil the property produced.
3. Granny prepared mustard greens and possum innards.
4. The Clampetts' dog's name was Duke.
5. Jed asked if Tom Mix lived in Beverly Hills.


## BEWITCHED

1. Samantha "met" Darrin (they bumped into each other) outside the Clark building.
2. Samantha told Darrin that she was a witch on their wedding night.
3. In the premiere Darrin says he's from Missouri.
4. Samantha does a number of things to prove to Darrin that she's a witch. She moves an ashtray, opens a window, and mixes Darrin a drink with the use of her magical powers.

## THE BOB NEWHART SHOW

1. Bob finally agrees to go on vacation, and the Hartleys head for New Orleans.
2. Bob's barber's name is Mel (Richard Stahl).
3. Mrs. Peterson's first name was Doris.

## CAR 54, WHERE ARE YOU?

1. Muldoon was a member of the Bronx Stamp Club.
2. "The fanciest place in the Bronx" was the Chi-Chi Club.
3. The sign read, "On or off duty, wear your gun."

## HERE'S LUCY

1. Richard Burton said that he'd never seen Disneyland.
2. He disguised himself as the plumber (Sam) and left unnoticed.
3. Lucy tried on "the ring" (Elizabeth's tremendous diamond) and couldn't get it off.

## I MARRIED JOAN

1. Joan played bridge with the girls every Monday afternoon.
2. The luncheon was at the Blue Room at the Hotel Pierre.
3. The members of the Executive Council of the Ladies Club were, in addition to Joan, Mildred, Mabel, Virginia and Ruth.
4. The names of the two St. Bernards were Hector and Tony.

## JULIA

1. Julia was interviewed by Mr. Coltin.
2. Julia lived in apartment #5, the Waggedorns in #2.
3. Earl said he would let Corey blow his whistle.
4. Julia made her calls from the drugstore.
5. Dick Privit was played by Lloyd Haynes of "Room 222" fame.

## LEAVE IT TO BEAVER

1. Beaver attended Grant Avenue School. The school psychologist was Dr. Wade.
2. Beaver wanted to be a garbageman because he wouldn't have to wash his hands and no one would care how he smelled.
3. Beaver's regular barber was Stanley. He charged $1.50.
4. Beaver and his pals talked to Don Drysdale on the phone.

## THE MANY LOVES OF DOBIE GILLIS

1. Both boys fell head over heels for Pearl Arnold.
2. Maynard received a hardship discharge (the army's hardship).

3. Dobie's dad owned Gillis' Groceries.
4. A "Subgum Sundae" cost a whopping 35¢.

## THE MARY TYLER MOORE SHOW

1. Ted and Georgette were married in Mary's apartment.
2. Georgette wore plaid to her spur-of-the-moment wedding.
3. Ted and Georgette were married by Rev. Chaffield, as played by John Ritter.
4. According to the premiere episode, Mary was a Presbyterian.
5. Mary drove a white Mustang to Minneapolis.
6. Ted's favorite Disney movie is *Snow White*.

## THE MUNSTERS

1. Herman wanted to join the Mockingbird Heights Country Club.
2. Grandpa had ten wives.
3. Herman fell apart when "Kukla, Fran and Ollie" was cancelled.

## MY THREE SONS

1. The door-to-door salesman was selling cosmetics.
2. Doreen Peters had a crush on Chip.
3. Steve dated Pamela McLish in the premiere episode.
4. Steve had been a widower for six years.
5. Both "Bub" and Pamela made pecan layer cake.

## THE PHIL SILVERS SHOW

1. Bilko's girl friend was Joan Hogan (Elizabeth Fraser). Her hometown was Sumter, South Carolina.
2. Sergeant Ritzik's wife's name was Emma.
3. The sign read, "Gentlemen playing cards for money do so at their own risk."

## THE REAL McCOYS

1. The McCoys inherited their ranch from Uncle Ben McCoy.
2. Upon their first meeting, Grandpa insists that Pepino is a Russian.
3. Grandpa would rather have seen Luke marry 16-year-old Elvira Goody from back home in West Virginia.

## TOPPER

1. The Kerbys took flight No. 6 to go on vacation.
2. They met Neil, their St. Bernard, on the ski slopes. (He was drunk!)
3. Neil was named after George's cousin.

# NOTE

In closing, we would just like to urge you to keep all
these great series fresh in your mind and help to keep
them alive in the minds of others. Through doing this book
we have once again realized what a great form of entertainment television once was and possibly can be again.
We owe a debt to all the stars and production crews that
have taken part in the classic series included in this book,
and we also acknowledge the same people from the not-
so-classic series listed within, for their shows gave birth
to possibly the most fascinating trivia questions of all.

Please feel free to drop us a note with your favorite
trivia questions. We are always thrilled to hear from our
readers! Knowing that there are people like us out there
who want to preserve these great memories makes us feel
just great!

Thanks!

# Acknowledgment

We would like to acknowledge the help and
cooperation of the staff at the Museum of Broadcasting,
who were a great help to us with our various research
projects in compiling the information contained in this
book.

# Index to Shows

ABBOTT & COSTELLO SHOW, THE, 105, 216, 242
ACCUSED, 15, 179
ADAM 12, 46, 193
ADAM'S RIB, 149
ADDAMS FAMILY, THE, 118, 223, 242
ADVENTURES OF CHAMPION, THE, 153–54, 241
ADVENTURES OF FU MANCHU, 158
ADVENTURES OF OZZIE & HARRIET, THE, 105, 166, 217, 246
ADVENTURES OF RIN TIN TIN, THE, 154, 241
ADVENTURES OF ROBIN HOOD, 41
ADVENTURES AT SCOTT ISLAND, 158
ADVENTURES OF SIR LANCELOT, 41
ALAN YOUNG SHOW, THE, 162, 245
ALCOA PREMIERE, 159, 243
ALCOA PRESENTS, 160, 243
ALFRED HITCHCOCK PRESENTS, 160, 244
ALIAS SMITH AND JONES, 63, 200
ALL IN THE FAMILY, 136, 151, 159, 162, 232
ALL'S FAIR, 136, 232
AMAZING MR. MALONE, 158
AMERICAN GIRLS, THE, 35, 188
AMERICANS, THE, 85, 209
AMOS 'N' ANDY, 105, 217
AMY PRENTISS, 46, 193
ANDROS TARGETS, THE, 99, 102, 215
ANDY GRIFFITH SHOW, THE, 118–19, 166, 223, 246
ANDY OF MAYBERRY, 223
ANGIE, 149
ANN SOTHERN SHOW, THE, 105–106, 217
ANNA AND THE KING, 149
ANNIE OAKLEY, 162
APPLE'S WAY, 89–90, 211
ARCHER, 74
ARMCHAIR DETECTIVE, 74
ARNIE, 136–37, 232
ARREST AND TRIAL, 158
ASPHALT JUNGLE, THE, 53

ASSIGNMENT VIENNA, 24, 158, 183
AVENGERS, THE, 24, 183

BAA BAA BLACK SHEEP, 85, 209
BACHELOR FATHER, 106, 162, 217, 242
BAD NEWS BEARS, THE, 137, 232
BADGE 714, 158
BAILEYS OF BALBOA, 132
BALL FOUR, 137, 233
BANACEK, 68, 202
BANYON, 68, 202
BARBARY COAST, THE, 64
BAREFOOT IN THE PARK, 137, 233
BARETTA, 47, 193, 242
BARNEY BLAKE, POLICE REPORTER, 158
BARNEY MILLER, 137–38, 233
BARON, THE, 25, 183
BAT MASTERSON, 57, 197–98
BATMAN, 42–43, 163, 191–92
BATTLESTAR GALACTICA, 76–77, 205, 242
BEACON HILL, 95
BEHIND CLOSED DOORS, 25, 183
BEN CASEY, 4–5, 7, 12, 175, 177
BERT D'ANGELO/SUPERSTAR, 53
BEST SELLERS, 186
BEULAH, 113
BEVERLY HILLBILLIES, THE, 133–34, 166–67, 231, 246
BEWITCHED, 119, 163, 167, 223, 246
BEYOND WESTWORLD, 77, 205
BIFF BAKER, U.S.A., 41
BIG EDDIE, 149
BIG HAWAII, 35, 188
BIG TOWN, 99, 102, 158, 215
BIG VALLEY, THE, 57, 198
BILL COSBY SHOW, THE, 119, 223–24
BILL DANA SHOW, THE, 119, 224
BING CROSBY SHOW, THE, 119–20, 224
BIONIC WOMAN, THE, 35, 188, 242
BLACK ROBE, THE, 15, 179
BLACK SADDLE, 64
BLANSKY'S BEAUTIES, 138, 233
BLONDIE, 106, 217
BLUE KNIGHT, THE, 47, 193
BLUE LIGHT, 25, 183

BOB & CAROL & TED & ALICE, 138, 233
BOB CRANE SHOW, THE, 138, 233
BOB CUMMINGS SHOW, THE, 106, 217
BOB NEWHART SHOW, THE, 138, 167, 233, 247
BOLD ONES, THE, 17, 177
BONANZA, 66, 201
BORN FREE, 35–36, 188
BOSS LADY, 113
BOSTON BLACKIE, 74
BOURBON STREET BEAT, 112
BRACKEN'S WORLD, 90, 211
BRADY BUNCH, THE, 120, 224, 242
BRANDED, 58, 198
BREAKING POINT, 5, 12, 175
BRIAN KEITH SHOW, THE, 139, 158, 233
BRIDGET LOVES BERNIE, 139, 234
BROKEN ARROW, 58, 198
BRONK, 68, 202
BROTHERS, THE, 113
BUCK ROGERS, 77, 206
BUCK ROGERS IN THE 25th CENTURY, 77, 206
BURKE'S LAW, 69, 159, 202
BURNS & ALLEN SHOW, THE, 161, 244
BUS STOP, 163
BUSTING LOOSE, 149

C.P.O. SHARKEY, 139, 234
CADE'S COUNTY, 47, 193
CAIN'S HUNDRED, 53
CALL OF THE WEST, 158
CALUCCI'S DEPARTMENT, 139, 234
CAMP RUNAMUCK, 132
CANNON, 69, 202
CAPTAIN NICE, 120, 224
CAR 54, WHERE ARE YOU?, 120, 167, 224, 247
CARIBE, 53
CARTER COUNTRY, 139–40, 234
CASABLANCA, 25, 184
CAVALCADE OF STARS, 115
CHARLIE'S ANGELS, 69, 202
CHASE, 53
CHECKMATE, 74
CHEYENNE, 58, 198
CHICAGO TEDDY BEARS, THE, 140, 234
CHICO AND THE MAN, 140, 234
CHINA SMITH, 41
CHIPS, 47, 193
CHISOLMS, THE, 64
CHOPPER ONE, 48, 193

CIMARRON STRIP, 58, 198
CIRCUS BOY, 41, 242
CISCO KID, THE, 64
CITY ASSIGNMENT, 158
CITY DETECTIVE, 53
CITY HOSPITAL, 5, 175
CITY OF ANGELS, 69, 202
COLT .45, 64
COLUMBO, 48, 194
COMBAT, 85–86, 209
COMBAT SERGEANT, 86, 209
CONVOY, 86, 209
COOL MILLION, 70, 202
CORNER BAR, THE, 140, 234
CORONET BLUE, 90, 211
COURT-MARTIAL, 95
COURT OF LAST RESORT, THE, 158
COURTSHIP OF EDDIE'S FATHER, THE, 121, 160, 224, 244
COWBOY THEATER, 160, 244
COWBOYS, THE, 64
CRIME PHOTOGRAPHER, 99, 102, 215
CRIME SYNDICATED, 175
CROSS CURRENT, 158
CROSS QUESTION, 181
CRUSADER, 25, 184
CUSTER, 64

D.A., THE, 15, 179
D.A.'S MAN, THE, 53
DAKTARI, 36, 188, 242
DAMON RUNYON THEATER, 160, 244
DAN AUGUST, 48, 194
DANGER MAN, 26, 184, 187
DANGEROUS ASSIGNMENT, 26, 184
DANIEL BOONE, 58, 198
DANNY THOMAS SHOW, THE, 107, 218
DANTE, 163
DAY IN COURT, 179
DEAR DETECTIVE, 74
DEATH VALLEY DAYS, 59, 158, 198
DEBBIE REYNOLDS SHOW, THE, 121, 224
DECEMBER BRIDE, 107, 159, 218
DEFENDERS, THE, 15–16, 179
DELPHI BUREAU, THE, 26, 184
DELVECCHIO, 48, 194
DENNIS THE MENACE, 107, 218
DESTRY, 64
DIANA, 141, 235
DICK TRACY, 53
DICK VAN DYKE SHOW, THE, 134–35, 150, 232

DIRTY SALLY, 64
DOC, 141, 235
DOC ELLIOTT, 6, 175–76
DOCTOR, THE, 6, 176
DOCTORS AND THE NURSES, THE, 178
DOCTORS' HOSPITAL, 6, 12, 176
DOCTORS' PRIVATE LIVES, 6, 176
DON RICKLES SHOW, THE, 141, 235
DONNA REED SHOW, THE, 107–108, 161, 218, 244
DOOR WITH NO NAME, 158, 184
DOORWAY TO DANGER, 26, 158, 184
DORIS DAY SHOW, THE, 121, 225, 243
DOUBLE LIFE OF HENRY PHYFE, 133
DR. HUDSON'S SECRET JOURNAL, 7, 176
DR. KILDARE, 7, 12, 160, 176, 244
DR. SIMON LOCKE, 7–8, 176
DRAGNET, 48–49, 158, 161, 194, 244
DUKE, THE, 74
DUMPLINGS, THE, 149
DUNDEE AND THE CULHANE, 64
DUSTY'S TRAIL, 149
DYNASTY, 185

EIGHT IS ENOUGH, 90, 211
87th PRECINCT, 53
EISCHIED, 49, 194
ELEVENTH HOUR, THE, 8, 176
EMERGENCY, 91, 211
EMPIRE, 159
ENSIGN O'TOOLE, 133
ESPIONAGE, 27, 184
EVE ARDEN SHOW, THE, 245
EXECUTIVE SUITE, 95
EXPOSE, 158

F.B.I., THE, 49, 194
F TROOP, 121, 225
FAMILY, 91, 211–12
FAMILY AFFAIR, 122, 225
FAMILY HOLVAK, THE, 91, 212
FARADAY AND COMPANY, 70, 203
FARMER'S DAUGHTER, THE, 122, 225
FATHER KNOWS BEST, 108, 178, 218
FAVORITE STORY, 160, 244
FELONY SQUAD, 53
FIBBER McGEE AND MOLLY, 108, 218

FITZPATRICKS, THE, 95
FIVE FINGERS, 27, 184
FLASH GORDON, 76, 77–78, 206
FLIPPER, 153, 154, 241
FLYING HIGH, 163
FLYING NUN, THE, 122, 225
FOR THE PEOPLE, 53
FOREIGN INTRIGUE, 27, 158, 184
FOUR IN ONE, 178
FROM HERE TO ETERNITY, 86, 209
FRONT PAGE, THE, 99, 102, 215
FRONT PAGE DETECTIVE, 99–100, 215
FRONTIER JUSTICE, 160, 244
FUGITIVE, THE, 96–97, 214
FUNNY FACE, 141, 159, 235

GALACTICA 1980, 205
GALE STORM SHOW, THE, 108, 158, 218
GALLANT MEN, THE, 86, 209
GALLERY OF MME. LUI-TSONG, THE, 158
GANGBUSTERS, 163, 245
GARRISON'S GORILLAS, 88, 210–11
GEMINI MAN, 41
GENE AUTREY SHOW, THE, 161, 244
GENERAL ELECTRIC THEATER, 160, 244
GENTLE BEN, 154, 241
GEORGE BURNS AND GRACIE ALLEN SHOW, THE, 108–109, 219
GET CHRISTIE LOVE, 54
GET SMART, 122–23, 225
GHOST AND MRS. MUIR, THE, 123, 226, 242
GHOST STORY, 160, 244
GIBBSVILLE, 95, 163
GIDGET, 123, 226
GILLIGAN'S ISLAND, 123, 163, 226
GIRL FROM U.N.C.L.E., THE, 27, 185
GOLDBERGS, THE, 109, 219
GOMER PYLE, U.S.M.C., 123–24, 226
GOOD GUYS, THE, 124, 226
GOOD HEAVENS, 163
GOOD LIFE, THE, 141–42, 235
GOOD MORNING, WORLD, 124, 226
GOOD TIMES, 159
GOVERNOR AND J.J., THE, 124, 226
GRANDPA GOES TO WASHINGTON, 142, 235

GRAY GHOST, 41
GREAT GILDERSLEEVE, THE, 109, 219
GREATEST SHOW ON EARTH, THE, 161, 244
GREEN ACRES, 124–25, 227, 242
GREEN HORNET, THE, 36, 163, 188, 245
GRIFF, 70, 203
GUNS OF WILL SONNETT, THE, 64
GUNSLINGER, 64
GUNSMOKE, 65, 66, 161, 163, 200, 244

HANK, 133
HAPPY DAYS, 142, 159, 235
HARBOR COMMAND, 54
HARBOURMASTER, 41, 158
HARRY-O, 70, 203
HATHAWAYS, THE, 133, 243
HAVE GUN WILL TRAVEL, 59, 198
HAVING BABIES, 8, 12, 177
HAWAII FIVE-O, 49, 194–95
HAWAIIAN EYE, 70–71, 203
HAWKINS, 16, 179–80
HAZEL, 125, 227
HE & SHE, 125, 227
HEADMASTER, 95
HEAVEN FOR BETSY, 113
HEC RAMSEY, 163
HENNESEY, 91, 212
HERE COME THE BRIDES, 92, 163, 212
HERE'S LUCY, 168, 228, 247
HEY LANDLORD, 125, 227
HIGH CHAPARRAL, 59, 199
HIGHWAY PATROL, 49, 195
HILL STREET BLUES, 194
HOGAN'S HEROES, 126, 227
HOLMES AND YOYO, 149
HONDO, 64
HONEY WEST, 71, 159, 203, 243
HONEYMOONERS, THE, 115–17, 151, 222–23, 243
HOPALONG CASSIDY, 64
HOT L BALTIMORE, 142, 236
HOTEL DE PAREE, 59, 199
HOW THE WEST WAS WON, 64, 245
HUNTER, 28
HUNTER, THE, 28, 185

I COVER TIMES SQUARE, 100, 215
I DREAM OF JEANNIE, 126, 227, 243
I LED THREE LIVES, 28, 185
I LOVE LUCY, 113–14, 221–22

I MARRIED JOAN, 109, 168, 219, 247
I SPY, 28–29, 185
I'M DICKENS—HE'S FENSTER, 126, 227
IMMORTAL, THE, 36, 163, 189
INTERNS, THE, 8, 12, 177
INVADERS, THE, 78, 206
INVISIBLE MAN (ADVENTURE), 41
INVISIBLE MAN, THE (INTRIGUE), 29, 185
IRON HORSE, THE, 64
IRONSIDE, 50, 159, 195
IT TAKES A THIEF, 29, 185–86
IT'S ABOUT TIME, 126, 228

JACKIE GLEASON SHOW, THE, 115
JAMES AT 15, 95
JAMIE, 113
JANET DEAN, REGISTERED NURSE, 9, 177
JEFFERSONS, THE, 159, 232
JERICHO, 87, 210
JIGSAW, 54
JIMMY STEWART SHOW, THE, 143, 236
JOANIE LOVES CHIACHI, 234
JOE AND SONS, 149
JOE FORRESTER, 50, 195
JOEY BISHOP SHOW, THE, 127, 228
JOHNNY RINGO, 64
JUDD FOR THE DEFENSE, 16, 21, 180
JULIA, 127, 168–69, 228, 247
JULIE FARR, M.D., 177
JUSTICE, 16, 180

KATE McSHANE, 16–17, 180
KAZ, 71, 203
KENTUCKY JONES, 163
KING OF DIAMONDS, 158
KINGSTON: CONFIDENTIAL, 100, 215
KIT CARSON, 64
KLONDIKE, 41
KODIAK, 54
KOJAK, 50, 195
KOLCHAK: THE NIGHT STALKER, 92, 212
KUKLA, FRAN, AND OLLIE, 247
KUNG FU, 63, 200–201

LANCER, 65
LAND OF THE GIANTS, 82–83, 208–209, 243
LANIGAN'S RABBI, 50, 195
LARAMIE, 65

LAREDO, 65
LASSIE, 153, 155, 241
LAW AND MR. JONES, THE, 17, 180
LAW OF PLAINSMAN, 65
LAWMAN, THE, 59, 199
LAWYERS, THE, 17, 180
LAZARUS SYNDROME, THE, 9, 12, 177
LEAVE IT TO BEAVER, 109–10, 169, 179, 219, 247
LET'S MAKE A DEAL, 152
LIFE AND LEGEND OF WYATT EARP, THE, 60, 199
LIFE AND TIMES OF GRIZZLY ADAMS, 41
LIFE OF RILEY, THE, 110, 219
LIFE WITH ELIZABETH, 163, 242
LIFE WITH FATHER, 110, 219
LINEUP, THE, 54
LITTLE PEOPLE, THE, 158
LOCK-UP, 17, 180
LOGAN'S RUN, 78, 206
LONE RANGER, THE, 60, 161, 199, 242, 244
LONG, HOT SUMMER, THE, 92, 212
LONGSTREET, 71, 203
LOST IN SPACE, 81–82, 208
LOTSA LUCK, 143, 236
LOU GRANT, 100, 102, 215
LOVE AMERICAN STYLE, 235
LOVE & MARRIAGE, 113
LOVE ON A ROOFTOP, 133
LOVE THAT BOB, 217
LUCAN, 37, 189
LUCAS TANNER, 92, 212
LUCY IN CONNECTICUT, 164
LUCY SHOW, THE, 127, 228

M*A*S*H*, 143, 151, 161, 177, 236, 244
M SQUAD, 50, 195
MacKENZIE'S RAIDERS, 65
MADIGAN, 51, 195
MAGICIAN, THE, 37, 189
MAJOR ADAMS, TRAILMASTER, 158
MAKE ROOM FOR DADDY, 218
MAMA, 110, 220
MAN AND THE CITY, 96
MAN CALLED SLOANE, A, 29, 186, 187
MAN CALLED X, THE, 30, 186
MAN FROM ATLANTIS, 37, 189
MAN FROM INTERPOL, 54
MAN FROM U.N.C.L.E., THE, 30, 185, 186, 187
MAN IN A SUITCASE, 74

MAN WHO NEVER WAS, THE, 30, 186
MAN WITH A CAMERA, 96
MAN WITHOUT A GUN, 65
MANHUNT, 54
MANHUNTER, THE, 72, 204
MANNIX, 72, 204
MANY HAPPY RETURNS, 164
MANY LOVES OF DOBIE GILLIS, THE, 110–11, 169, 220, 247
MARCUS WELBY, M.D., 12, 13, 178
MARK SABER, 74
MARRIAGE, THE, 113
MARSHAL OF GUNSIGHT PASS, THE, 65
MARTIN KANE, PRIVATE EYE, 74, 158
MARY TYLER MOORE SHOW, THE, 150–51, 169–70, 240, 248
MASK, THE, 158
MATT HELM, 72, 204
MATT LINCOLN, 9, 177
MAUDE, 143, 159, 232, 236
MAVERICK, 60, 164, 199
MAYA, 38, 189
MAYBERRY, R.F.D., 127, 228
McCLOUD, 51, 195
McCOY, 72, 204
McCOYS, THE, 221
McHALE'S NAVY, 128, 228
McLEAN STEVENSON SHOW, THE, 144, 236
McMILLAN AND WIFE, 51, 195
ME AND THE CHIMP, 150, 242
MEDIC, 9, 161, 177, 244
MEDICAL CENTER, 9–10, 177
MEET CORLISS ARCHER, 113
MEET MILLIE, 113
MEN, THE, 183
MEN AT LAW, 181
MEN FROM SHILOH, THE, 158
MEN INTO SPACE, 164
MICKEY, 128, 228
MILLIONAIRE, THE, 164
MISSION IMPOSSIBLE, 32–33, 187
MOBILE ONE, 38, 189
MOD SQUAD, THE, 51, 196
MONA McCLUSKEY, 133
MONKEES, THE, 128, 229
MONROES, THE, 60, 199, 243
MORK & MINDY, 144, 236
MOSES—THE LAWGIVER, 164
MOST DEADLY GAME, THE, 72–73, 204
MOST WANTED, 54
MOTHERS-IN-LAW, THE, 129, 229
MR. BROADWAY, 96
MR. DEEDS GOES TO TOWN, 133
MR. DISTRICT ATTORNEY, 54

MR. ED, 155, 241
MR. LUCKY, 37, 189
MR. NOVAK, 93, 212
MR. PEEPERS, 111, 220
MR. ROBERTS, 164
MR. TERRIFIC, 128, 229
MUNSTERS, THE, 129, 170, 224, 229, 242, 248
MY FAVORITE MARTIAN, 129, 229
MY FRIEND FLICKA, 154, 242
MY FRIEND IRMA, 111, 220
MY FRIEND TONY, 74
MY LITTLE MARGIE, 111, 220
MY LIVING DOLL, 129, 229
MY MOTHER THE CAR, 130, 229
MY THREE SONS, 130, 164, 170, 230, 242, 248
MY WORLD AND WELCOME TO IT, 130, 230
MYSTERIES OF CHINATOWN, 158

N.Y.P.D., 51, 196
NAKED CITY, 52, 196
NAKIA, 54
NAME OF THE GAME, THE, 38, 190
NANCY DREW MYSTERIES, THE, 38, 190
NANCY WALKER SHOW, THE, 144, 237
NANNY AND THE PROFESSOR, 144, 237, 242
NATIONAL VELVET, 243
NEEDLES AND PINS, 150
NEW ADVENTURES OF PERRY MASON, THE, 182–83
NEW ANDY GRIFFITH SHOW, THE, 145, 237
NEW AVENGERS, THE, 183
NEW BREED, THE, 54
NEW DICK VAN DYKE SHOW, THE, 145, 237
NEW DOCTORS, THE, 10, 12, 177–78
NICHOLS, 65
NO TIME FOR SERGEANTS, 130, 230
NOAH'S ARK, 10, 178
NORBY, 164
NOT FOR PUBLICATION, 100, 102, 216
NURSE, 11, 12, 178
NURSES, THE, 11, 12, 178

O.K. CRACKERBY, 133
O.S.S., 87, 210
OCCASIONAL WIFE, 133

ODD COUPLE, THE, 151–52, 235, 240
OH, SUSANNA, 158
O'HARA, U.S. TREASURY, 54
OMNIBUS, 160, 244
ON OUR OWN, 150
ON THE ROCKS, 145, 237
ONCE AN EAGLE, 87, 210
OPERATION PETTICOAT, 145, 237
OREGON TRAIL, THE, 65
OUR MISS BROOKS, 111–12, 163, 220
OUT OF THE BLUE, 159
OUTER LIMITS, 78, 206
OUTLAWS, THE, 65
OVERLAND TRAIL, 60, 199
OWEN MARSHALL, COUNSELOR AT LAW, 17–18, 180–81

PAPER CHASE, THE, 93, 161, 213, 244
PAPER MOON, 145–46, 237
PARIS, 54
PARIS 7000, 164
PARTRIDGE FAMILY, THE, 146, 161, 238, 242, 244
PASSPORT TO DANGER, 30, 186
PATTY DUKE SHOW, THE, 131, 230
PAUL LYNDE SHOW, THE, 146, 238
PAUL SAND IN FRIENDS AND LOVERS, 146, 238
PEOPLE'S CHOICE, THE, 112, 220, 243
PERRY MASON, 21–22, 182–83
PERSUADERS, THE, 39, 190
PETE AND GLADYS, 133, 159
PETROCELLI, 18, 21, 181
PETTICOAT JUNCTION, 131, 230
PEYTON PLACE, 93, 164, 213
PHIL SILVERS SHOW, THE, 112, 151, 170–71, 221, 248
PHOTOCRIME, 159
PHYLLIS, 146–47, 238
PLACE THE FACE, 175
PLANET OF THE APES, THE, 78–79, 206
PLEASE DON'T EAT THE DAISIES, 131, 230, 242
POLICE SURGEON, 176
POLICE WOMAN, 52, 196
POPI, 147, 238
PRACTICE, THE, 150, 164
PRISONER, THE, 159
PRIVATE SECRETARY, 113
PROFESSIONAL FATHER, 164
PRUITTS OF SOUTHAMPTON, THE, 164

PSYCHIATRIST, THE, 11, 178
PUBLIC DEFENDER, THE, 18, 181

QUARK, 150

RACKET SQUAD, 54
RAFFERTY, 11, 12, 178
RAMAR OF THE JUNGLE, 41
RANGE RIDER, THE, 63
RANGO, 133
RAT PATROL, THE, 87, 210
RAWHIDE, 61, 199
RAY MILLAND SHOW, THE, 164
REAL McCOYS, THE, 112, 171,
    221, 248
REDIGO, 159
RENDEZVOUS, 31, 186
REPORTER, THE, 100–101, 102,
    216
RESTLESS GUN, THE, 65
RHINEMANN EXCHANGE, THE,
    31, 186
RHODA, 147, 238
RICHIE BROCKELMAN,
    PRIVATE EYE, 159
RIFLEMAN, THE, 61, 199–200
RIVERBOAT, 165
ROAD WEST, THE, 65
ROARING TWENTIES, THE, 101,
    102, 216
ROCKFORD FILES, THE, 159
ROOKIES, THE, 52, 196
ROOM 222, 93, 213, 247
ROPERS, THE, 243
ROSETTI AND RYAN, 18, 181
ROUTE 66, 39, 190
ROY ROGERS SHOW, THE, 161,
    243, 244
RUN FOR YOUR LIFE, 39, 190

S.W.A.T., 52, 196
SAINT, THE, 31, 187
SAINTS AND SINNERS, 101, 102,
    216
SAM, 54
SAM BENEDICT, 19, 21, 181
SAN FRANCISCO
    INTERNATIONAL AIRPORT, 94,
    213
SAN PEDRO BEACH BUMS, THE,
    165
SANDY DUNCAN SHOW, THE,
    159
SANFORD AND SON, 147, 238
SARGE, 94, 159, 213
SCHLITZ PLAYHOUSE OF
    STARS, 160, 244
SEA HUNT, 39, 190
SECOND HUNDRED YEARS,
    THE, 131, 230

SECRET AGENT, 31, 159, 187
SERGEANT PRESTON OF THE
    YUKON, 243
SERPICO, 54
77 SUNSET STRIP, 73, 204
SHADOW OF THE CLOAK, 32, 187
SHAFT, 73, 204
SHANE, 61, 200
SHEENA, QUEEN OF THE
    JUNGLE, 165
SHIRLEY, 242
SHOTGUN SLADE, 65
SILENT FORCE, THE, 54
SILVER THEATER, 160, 244
SIX MILLION DOLLAR MAN,
    THE, 39–40, 190
SIXTH SENSE, 96
SKAG, 94, 213
SLATTERY'S PEOPLE, 165
SMITH FAMILY, THE, 94, 213
SMOTHERS BROTHERS SHOW,
    THE, 165
SNOOP SISTERS, THE, 73, 204
SPACE—1999, 79, 207
STANLEY, 113
STAR TREK, 79, 207
STARSKY AND HUTCH, 52, 196
STEVE CANYON, 41
STOCKARD CHANNING IN JUST
    FRIENDS, 147–48, 239
STONEY BURKE, 65
STOREFRONT LAWYERS, 19, 21,
    181
STRANGER, THE, 159
STREETS OF SAN FRANCISCO,
    53, 197
STUDIO ONE, 16
SUGAR TIME!, 165
SUPER, THE, 150
SUPERMAN, 43–44, 192
SURFSIDE SIX, 159
SURVIVORS, THE, 165
SUSPICION, 160, 244
SWISS FAMILY ROBINSON, THE,
    40, 190–91
SWITCH, 73–74, 205

T.H.E. CAT, 40, 191
TABITHA, 148, 239
TAMMY, 132, 231
TARGET: THE CORRUPTORS,
    101, 158, 216
TARZAN, 40, 191, 243
TELLTALE CLUE, THE, 54
TEMPERATURES RISING, 148, 239
TENAFLY, 74, 205
THAT GIRL, 132, 231
THAT WONDERFUL GUY, 113
THEN CAME BRONSON, 40, 191
THEY STAND ACCUSED, 19, 181

THIN MAN, THE, 75, 205
THIRD MAN, THE, 32, 187
TIGHTROPE, 54
TIME EXPRESS, THE, 165, 246
TIME TUNNEL, THE, 82, 208
TO ROME WITH LOVE, 132, 231
TOMA, 53, 197
TOMBSTONE TERRITORY, 65
TONY RANDALL SHOW, THE, 148, 239
TOPPER, 112–13, 171, 221, 242, 248
TRACKDOWN, 159
TRAFFIC COURT, 19, 182
TREASURY MEN IN ACTION, 159
TRIALS OF O'BRIEN, 20, 21, 182
TWELVE O'CLOCK HIGH, 87–88, 210
20TH CENTURY-FOX HOUR, 160, 244
TWILIGHT ZONE, THE, 79–80, 207
240-ROBERT, 41, 191

UFO, 80, 207
UGLIEST GIRL IN TOWN, 133
UNTOUCHABLES, THE, 55, 197

VALENTINE'S DAY, 133
VERDICT IS YOURS, THE, 20, 182
VIRGINIAN, THE, 61, 158, 200
VOYAGE TO THE BOTTOM OF THE SEA, 80–81, 208

W.E.B., 96
WACKIEST SHIP IN THE ARMY, THE, 88, 210
WAGON TRAIN, 62, 158, 200
WALTONS, THE, 95, 214
WANTED: DEAD OR ALIVE, 62, 159, 200
WARNER BROTHERS PRESENTS, 160, 244
WAVERLY WONDERS, THE, 148, 239
WELCOME BACK KOTTER, 149, 239
WEST POINT STORY, 160, 244
WESTSIDE MEDICAL, 12, 178
WHEN THINGS WERE ROTTEN, 149, 239
WHITE SHADOW, THE, 95, 214
WILD BILL HICKOK, 64
WILD, WILD WEST, THE, 62, 200
WILLY, 20, 21, 182
WIRE SERVICE, 101, 216
WITNESS, THE, 20, 182

YANCY DERRINGER, 41
YOU'LL NEVER GET RICH, 221
YOUNG DAN'L BOONE, 41

ZORRO, 62, 200, 242

# Index to Actors' Names

Aaker, Lee, 241
Abbott, Philip, 194
Acker, Sharon, 183
Ackerman, Bettye, 175
Adams, Don, 224
Adams, Mason, 215
Adams, Nick, 216
Adler, William, 216
Albert, Eddie, 205
Albertson, Jack, 176, 234, 235
Aletter, Frank, 228
Allen, Elizabeth, 234
Ames, Leon, 219
Ames, Willie, 191
Amos, John, 240
Amsterdam, Morey, 232
Anderson, Richard, 214
Anderson, Warner, 54
Anderson, Wayne, 93
Andrews, Stanley, 198
Andrews, Tige, 196
Andrews, Tod, 41
Androsky, Carol, 235
Ansara, Michael, 65, 198
Archer, Anne, 233
Arden, Eve, 129, 163
Arkin, David, 181
Armstrong, Bess, 149
Arness, James, 64, 66, 163, 245
Arnold, Pearl, 247
Asner, Ed, 240
Astaire, Fred, 186, 243
Astin, John, 192, 227, 237, 240
Ayres, Lew, 244
Azzara, Candy, 139, 234

Bailey, Raymond, 231
Bain, Barbara, 187, 207
Bain, Conrad, 236
Baker, Joe Don, 194
Ball, Lucille, 114
Bank, Frank, 219
Bankhead, Tallulah, 192
Banner, John, 234
Bari, Lynn, 113
Barnes, Joanna, 182
Barnes, Priscilla, 188
Barnstable, Cyb, 149
Barnstable, Tricia, 149
Baron, Sandy, 227
Barry, Gene, 190, 197, 202
Barry, J.J., 234
Barton, Jim, 233
Basehart, Richard, 208
Baxter, Anne, 179
Baxter, Meredith, 234
Beckman, Henry, 212

Bellamy, Ralph, 176, 179, 185, 204, 244
Bellwood, Pamela, 95
Benaderet, Bea, 230, 231
Bendix, William, 199, 219
Benedict, Dirk, 193
Benjamin, Richard, 227
Benton, Barbi, 246
Berle, Milton, 192, 225
Bernardi, Hershel, 232
Berry, Ken, 228
Bessell, Ted, 231
Besser, Joe, 216
Bethune, Zina, 178
Bettger, Lyle, 158
Betz, Carl, 180, 218
Billingsley, Barbara, 245
Birney, David, 54, 234
Bishop, Ed, 207
Bishop, Joey, 127, 228
Bixby, Bill, 189, 224, 229
Black, Marianne, 246
Blackman, Honor, 183
Blake, Madge, 228
Blake, Whitney, 227
Blondell, Joan, 212
Bonaduce, Danny, 238
Bond, Ward, 200
Boone, Richard, 177, 198
Bowen, Roger, 232
Braddock, Mickey, 41
Bradford, Richard, 74
Brady, Scott, 65
Brain, David, 189
Bramley, Raymond, 184
Brand, Neville, 65, 197
Brandan, Gavin, 179
Breck, Peter, 64, 198
Brennan, Walter, 64, 171
Breslin, Pat, 220
Brewster, Diane, 214
Bridges, Lloyd, 190, 195, 213
Britton, Pamela, 217, 229
Broderick, James, 212
Brolin, James, 178
Bronkov, Anex, 202
Bronson, Charles, 95
Brooks, Geraldine, 149
Broom, Sam, 176
Brophy, Kevin, 189
Brown, Chelsea, 177
Brown, John, 219
Brown, Peter, 199
Brown, Robert, 212
Browne, Carol, 246
Browne, Roscoe Lee, 204
Buchanan, Edgar, 230
Buckley, Betty, 211

Buckner, Susan, 190
Buktenica, Ray, 238
Bulifant, Joyce, 224
Buntrock, Bobby, 227
Buono, Victor, 192
Burke, Paul, 178, 210
Burr, Ann, 175
Burr, Raymond, 182, 194
Burton, Richard, 168, 247
Buttons, Red, 133
Byington, Spring, 218
Byrd, Ralph, 53

Cabot, Sebastian, 244
Cady, Frank, 227
Callan, Michael, 133
Cameron, Rod, 54
Campanella, Joseph, 180
Campos, Victor, 176
Canary, David, 201
Canfield, Mary Grace, 227
Cannon, J.D., 214
Carey, MacDonald, 180
Carey, Michele, 186
Carey, Olive, 180
Carey, Ron, 234
Carlson, Linda, 178
Carlson, Richard, 65, 185
Carlyle, Richard, 215
Carmel, Roger, 229
Carney, Art, 115, 192, 195
Carr, Darleen, 213
Carr, Didi, 246
Carradine, David, 200
Carrol, Diahann, 127
Carroll, Leo G., 30, 185, 221
Carroll, Pat, 218
Carroll, Robert, 158
Carter, Conlon, 180
Cartwright, Angela, 207, 218
Casey, Lawrence, 210
Cass, Peggy, 133
Cassidy, David, 238
Cassidy, Jack, 227
Cassidy, Joanna, 191
Chamberlain, Richard, 176
Champlin, Irene, 206
Chastain, Don, 121
Childress, Alvin, 217
Cioffi, Charles, 183
Clark, Fred, 219
Clinger, Debra, 188
Coates, Phyllis, 192
Cobb, Julie, 179
Coco, James, 234
Colbert, Robert, 208
Cole, Michael, 196
Collins, Gary, 96, 188, 210
Collins, Joan, 192
Collins, Stephen, 186

Compton, John, 53
Connelly, Christopher, 237
Connors, Chuck, 198, 200
Connors, Mike, 54, 204
Conrad, Michael, 194
Conrad, Robert, 74, 85, 179, 183, 186, 200, 203, 209
Conrad, William, 202, 214
Conreid, Hans, 239
Considine, Tim, 230
Constantine, Michael, 213
Converse, Frank, 196, 211
Convy, Bert, 204
Conway, Gary, 209
Conway, Pat, 65
Conway, Shirley, 178
Conway, Tim, 133
Conway, Tom, 74
Cooke, Alistair, 244
Cooper, Jackie, 189, 212
Coppage, Marc, 228
Corbett, Glen, 190
Corey, Wendell, 54, 176
Cosby, Bill, 185
Cotton, Joseph, 244
Cowan, Jerome, 216
Cox, Ronny, 211
Craig, Yvonne, 191
Crawford, Broderick, 158, 177, 195
Crawford, Johnny, 200
Crenna, Richard, 221, 232, 246
Croft, Mary Jane, 245
Cromwell, James, 236
Cronyn, Hume, 113
Crosby, Bing, 224
Crothers, Scatman, 152
Crough, Suzanne, 238
Crowley, Patricia, 195
Culp, Robert, 185
Cumbuka, Ji-Tu, 186
Cummings, Robert, 229
Curtis, Barry, 241
Curtis, Keene, 189
Curtis, Ken, 201
Curtis, Tony, 190, 204

Dailey, Dan, 226
Dalton, Abby, 212, 228
Daly, James, 177, 184
Daly, John, 215
Dana, Bill (Jose Jimenez), 227
Daniels, William, 224, 237
Danner, Blythe, 149
Dantine, Helmut, 187
Darling, Joan, 180
Darren, David, 208
Davis, Gail, 245
Davis, Joan, 219
Davis, Mimi, 187
Davis, Roger, 200

Day, Doris, 225
Deacon, Richard, 229, 232
DeCamp, Rosemary, 217, 219
DeFore, Don, 227
Dehner, John, 188, 225
Dekova, Frank, 225
Delany, Pat, 190
Dell, Gabriel, 234
DeLuise, Dom, 143, 236
Demarest, William, 113
Denning, Richard, 195
Denver, Bob, 220, 226
DeWilde, Brandon, 113, 200
DeWolfe, Billy, 226
Dey, Susan, 238
Dhiegh, Khigh, 195
Dibbs, Kem, 206
Dickinson, Angie, 196
Dietrich, Dena, 150, 245
Diller, Phyllis, 245
Dillman, Bradford, 96
Dinehart, Mason Alan, 199
Dixon, Ivan, 126
Dolenz, Micky, 229
Dolye, David, 202
Donahue, Elinor, 223
Donlevy, Brian, 184
Doohan, James, 207
Douglas, Fergus McBain, 245
Douglas, Melvyn, 244
Douglas, Michael, 197
Dowdell, Robert, 206
Drew, Paula, 215
Drury, James, 200
Duel, Peter, 132, 200
Duff, Howard, 53, 245
Duffy, Patrick, 189
Dukes, David, 95
Dumont, Margaret, 220
Duncan, Sandy, 235
Dunn, Michael, 200
Dunne, Irene, 244
Duryea, Dan, 41

Eastwood, Clint, 199
Edelman, Herb, 226
Edwards, Vince, 175, 177, 186
Eggar, Samantha, 150
Eisley, Anthony, 203
Elcar, Dana, 209
Elizondo, Hector, 238
Elliot, Jane, 181
Elliott, Sam, 210
Ely, Ron, 191
Erickson, Leif, 199
Estrada, Eric, 193
Evans, Linda, 185, 198, 217
Evans, Maurice, 223
Everett, Chad, 177
Ewell, Tom, 193

Fabares, Shelley, 233
Falk, Peter, 182, 194
Farentino, James, 180, 202
Farrell, Mike, 177
Farrow, Mia, 213
Fawcett-Majors, Farrah, 202, 211
Faylen, Frank, 220
Ferdin, Pamela, 240
Ferrer, Jose, 186
Fridell, Squire, 181
Field, Sally, 122, 200
Fisher, Gail, 204
Fleming, Eric, 199
Flynn, Joe, 128
Ford, Glenn, 193, 212
Ford, Paul, 133
Ford, Peter, 193
Forrest, Steve, 183, 196
Forster, Robert, 54, 202
Forsythe, John, 202, 231
Foster, Brian, 238
Foster, Jodie, 237
Fox, Bernard, 245
Foxworth, Robert, 181
Franciosa, Tony, 133, 190, 204
Francis, Anne, 203
Franciscus, James, 175, 185, 203, 212
Francks, Don, 87
Franz, Edward, 175
Frawley, William, 221, 230
Frazer, Elizabeth, 248
Frazier, Shiela, 177
Fredericks, Dean, 41
Fredericks, Richard, 240
Freeman, Kathleen, 236
French, Victor, 234
Friebus, Florida, 220, 233

Gallo, Mario, 194
Gargan, William, 74
Garland, Beverly, 224
Garner, James, 65, 199
Gautier, Dick, 225, 239
Gavin, John, 64, 176, 209
Gazzara, Ben, 158, 190
Gelbwaks, Jeremy, 238
George, Anthony, 74
George, Chris, 210
George, Christopher, 163, 189
George, Lynda Day, 187
Gerard, Gil, 206
Gerritsen, Lisa, 230
Ghostley, Alice, 224, 228
Gilford, Jack, 238
Gillette, Anita, 150, 233
Ging, Jack, 176
Glasner, Paul Michael, 196
Gleason, Jackie, 115, 219
Gless, Sharon, 205
Goddard, Mark, 208

Goldman, Danny, 235
Golonka, Arlene, 228
Gordon, Bruce, 183, 197
Gordon, Gale, 113, 218
Gordon, Glen, 158
Gorshin, Frank, 192
Gossett, Louis, Jr., 177
Gould, Sandra, 223
Goulet, Robert, 183
Graham, Ronny, 233
Graves, Peter, 187
Graves, Teresa, 53
Greaza, Walter, 159
Green, John, 179
Green, Shecky, 209
Greene, Lorne, 203, 205
Greene, Richard, 41
Grier, Roosevelt, 198
Griffin, Stephanie, 219
Griffith, Andy, 95, 237
Guardino, Harry, 183, 216
Gulager, Clu, 197, 213
Gunn, Moses, 64
Gwynne, Fred, 120

Hack, Shelly, 202
Hackett, Buddy, 113
Hackett, Joan, 179
Hadley, Reed, 54, 181
Haggard, Merle, 198
Haggerty, Dan, 41
Hagman, Larry, 235
Haid, Charles, 194
Hale, Alan, Jr., 41, 226
Hale, Barbara, 182
Hall, Jon, 41
Hall, Monty, 244
Hamilton, Bernie, 196
Hamilton, George, 245
Hamilton, John, 192
Hamilton, Lyn, 238
Hamilton, Neil, 113, 192
Harland, Robert, 216
Harmon, Mark, 54, 191
Harper, Ron, 206, 211
Harris, Jonathan, 208
Harris, Julie, 212
Harris, Phil, 225
Harris, Robert H., 219
Harrison, Gregory, 206
Hart, John, 199
Hartman, David, 177, 212
Hartman, Lisa, 239
Harty, Patricia, 217
Hatch, Richard, 197, 205
Havoc, June, 182
Hawn, Goldie, 226
Hayden, Don, 220
Hayden, Russell, 65
Hayes, Helen, 204

Haynes, Lloyd, 213, 247
Hedison, David, 184, 208
Henning, Linda Kaye, 230
Hensley, Pamela, 179
Hershey, Barbara, 209
Hill, Arthur, 180
Hill, Steven, 187
Hinton, Ed, 185
Hirsch, Judd, 194
Holland, Steve, 206
Holliman, Earl, 199
Hooks, Robert, 196
Hoover, Bubba, 238
Hopper, William, 182
Horne, Marilyn, 240
Horton, Edward Everett, 225
Horton, Richard, 200
Hotchkiss, Joan, 230
Houseman, John, 213
Howard, Andrea, 150
Howard, Clint, 241
Howard, John, 176
Howard, Ken, 204, 214
Howard, Ron, 213
Howard, Susan, 181
Huber, Harold, 215
Hudson, Rock, 196
Hughes, Bernard, 235
Hunt, Helen, 193
Hurst, Rick, 237
Huston, John, 186
Hutchins, Will, 217, 227
Hutton, Gunilla, 230
Hutton, Lauren, 186

Ingels, Marty, 227
Irwin, Wynn, 236
Ives, Burl, 133, 180

Jackson, Jay, 222
Jackson, Kate, 196, 202
Jackson, Mary, 214
Jackson, Sammy, 230
Jaffe, Sam, 175
Saint James, Susan, 196
Janis, Conrad, 236
Janssen, David, 54, 203, 214
Jason, Rick, 209
Jeffreys, Anne, 184
Jones, Davey, 229
Jones, Dean, 133, 234
Jones, Edgar Allen, Jr., 179, 182
Jones, Gordon, 216
Jones, James Earl, 54
Jory, Victor, 54
Jostyn, Jay, 54
Joyce, Elaine, 202

Kallman, Dick, 132
Kastner, Peter, 133

Kavner, Julie, 238
Kaye, Caren, 233
Kaye, Stubby, 113
Keach, Stacy, 53
Kearns, Joseph, 218
Keating, Larry, 219
Keith, Brian, 74, 139, 184, 225, 233
Keith, Richard, 221
Keith, Ronald, 219
Kelley, DeForrest, 207
Kelly, Brian, 241
Kelly, Jack, 199
Kennedy, George, 193, 213
Kennedy, John Milton, 74
Kerwin, Lance, 96
Ketchum, Dave, 133
Khan, Sajid, 189
Kincaid, Chet, 223
King, Wright, 200
Kirk, Joe, 216
Kirk, Phyllis, 205
Kitt, Eartha, 192
Kleeb, Helen, 214
Komack, James, 224
Kopell, Bernie, 225, 239
Kramer, Bert, 95
Kristen, Marta, 208
Kulp, Nancy, 231

Ladd, Cheryl, 202
Laire, Judson, 220
Lake, Arthur, 217
Lancaster, Burt, 245
Landau, Martin, 187, 207
Landesberg, Steve, 238
Landon, Michael, 201
Langdon, Sue Ann, 232
Lange, Hope, 237
Lansing, Robert, 53, 186, 210
Larkin, Sheila, 181
Larsen, Keith, 185
Larson, Jack, 192
Lawford, Peter, 205
Lawrence, Francine, 226
Lawrence, Letitia, 211
Leachman, Cloris, 241
Learned, Michael, 178
Lee, Bruce, 188, 203
Lehman, Lillian, 205
Lenihan, Deirdre, 149
Lewis, Al, 224
Lewis, Cathy, 220
Leyton, John, 87
Liebman, Ron, 203
Linville, Larry, 235
Lipton, Peggy, 196
Little, Cleavon, 239
Lockhart, June, 208, 241
Loeb, Philip, 219
Long, Richard, 198, 237

Lord, Jack, 65, 194
Lord, Phillips S., 245
Lowe, Edmund, 215
Lowry, Judith, 238
Luckinbill, Laurence, 184
Ludigan, William, 245
Lupino, Ida, 245
Lupton, John, 198
Lupus, Peter, 187
Lynde, Paul, 239
Lynley, Carol, 245

MacArthur, James, 194
MacGibbon, Harriet, 231
MacLane, Barton, 65
MacLeod, Gavin, 240
MacMurray, Fred, 164
Macnee, Patrick, 183
MacRae, Meredith, 230
Maharis, George, 190, 204
Mahoney, Jock, 41
Majors, Lee, 180, 190, 198
Malden, Karl, 197, 213
Mantooth, Randolph, 211
March, Hal, 219
Marchand, Nancy, 215
Markham, Monte, 133, 183
Marie, Rose, 232
Marshall, Don, 209
Marshall, E. G., 177
Martin, Pamela Sue, 190
Martin, Ross, 189, 200
Martin, Strother, 180
Marvin, Lee, 195
Mase, Marino, 87
Massey, Ilona, 186
Massey, Raymond, 176
Masur, Richard, 236
Matchett, Christine, 181
Maunder, Wayne, 64
May, Bob, 208
May, Donald, 216, 244
McCalla, Irish, 246
McCallum, David, 41, 186
McCambridge, Mercedes, 216
McClanahan, Rue, 236
McClory, Sean, 180
McClure, Doug, 64, 199
McClure, Frank Chandler, 182
McCord, Kent, 193
McCraw, Charles, 184
McDowall, Roddy, 186, 192, 206
McGavin, Darren, 92, 215
McGiver, John, 164, 229
McGoohan, Patrick, 178, 184, 187
McKay, Jim, 182
McMullan, Jim, 193
McNally, Stephen, 216
McNear, Howard, 223
McNichol, Kristy, 91, 211

McQueen, Steve, 200
Meadows, Audrey, 115
Meadows, Jayne, 177
Meara, Anne, 180, 238
Melton, Sid, 218, 227
Melville, Sam, 196
Menjou, Adolphe, 244
Meredith, Burgess, 192, 212
Meriweather, Lee, 192, 208, 237
Merman, Ethel, 192
Merrill, Gary, 158
Metrano, Art, 234
Michel, Franny, 211
Milland, Ray, 164, 246
Miller, Marvin, 158, 245
Mills, Donna, 235
Mills, John, 64
Milner, Martin, 190, 193
Mimieux, Yvette, 204
Mitchell, Don, 195
Mitchell, Cameron, 199
Mitchell, Scoey, 233
Mohr, Gerald, 184
Molinaro, Al, 235
Montgomery, Belinda, 189
Moody, King, 225
Moore, Barbara, 186
Moore, Clayton, 199
Moore, Mary Tyler, 150
Moore, Roger, 187, 190, 245
Moorehead, Agnes, 119, 207
Moran, Erin, 188
Morgan, Harry, 133, 179, 194
Morita, Pat, 235
Morrill, Priscilla, 240
Morris, Greg, 187
Morrow, Karen, 239
Morrow, Vic, 209
Morse, Barry, 207
Moses, Rich, 41
Muldaur, Diana, 188, 195
Mulhere, Edward, 226
Mullaney, Jack, 228
Mumy, Billy, 208
Murphy, Ben, 41, 200
Murphy, Diane, 223
Murphy, Erin, 223
Murton, Lionel, 210
Musante, Tony, 197

Nagel, Conrade, 244
Naismith, Laurence, 190
Namath, Joe, 239
Nash, Joe, 206
Natwick, Mildred, 204
Naughton, James, 206
Neill, Noel, 192
Neilsen, Leslie, 54, 211
Nelson, Barry, 185
Nelson, Ed, 54, 176

Nesmith, Mike, 229
Newell, Patrick, 183
Newland, John, 243
Newman, Barry, 181
Newmar, Julie, 129, 192
Nicholas, Denise, 213
Nigh, James, 215
Nimoy, Leonard, 187, 207
Nolan, Jeanette, 64
Nolan, Kathy, 221
Nolan, Lloyd, 197
North, Jay, 189
North, Sheree, 149
Nye, Louis, 217, 231

Oakland, Simon, 197
O'Brien, Edmond, 181, 212
O'Brien, Hugh, 199
O'Connell, Arthur, 230
O'Connor, Tim, 206
O'Donnell, Gene, 159
Ogilvy, Ian, 187
O'Herlihy, Dan, 212
O'Keefe, Dennis, 244
O'Keefe, Paul, 230
O'Loughlin, Gerald S., 196
Olson, Eric, 191
Olson, Nancy, 215
O'Neal, Ryan, 245
Oppenheimer, Alan, 190
Osmond, Ken, 219

Padilla, Manuel, Jr., 191
Parker, Fess, 198
Pastene, Robert, 206
Patterson, Hank, 227
Patterson, Melody, 225
Patterson, Neva, 176
Payne, John, 65
Pearce, Alice, 223
Peppard, George, 176, 202
Pepper, Barbara, 227
Pera, Radames, 201
Perez, Jose, 237
Perry, John Bennett, 191
Persoff, Nehemiah, 197
Pescow, Donna, 149
Peters, Bernadette, 232
Peyser, Penny, 239
Pitts, Zazu, 218
Pons, Bea, 224
Porter, Michael, 191
Porter, Sandy, 179
Potts, Cliff, 188, 210
Powers, Stefanie, 185
Preminger, Otto, 192
Prentis, Lou, 206
Prentiss, Paula, 227
Preston, Robert, 64
Preston, Wayde, 64

Price, Vincent, 192, 246
Provine, Dorothy, 216
Provost, Tom, 241
Prowse, Juliet, 133
Pyle, Denver, 231

Quayle, Anthony, 245
Quinn, Anthony, 95

Rainer, Ella, 177
Randall, Tony, 148, 220
Randolph, Joyce, 115
Randolph, Lillian, 217, 224
Rasey, Jean, 190
Raymond, Gary, 210
Read, Robert, 178
Reagan, Ronald, 198, 244
Reason, Rex, 65, 216
Redford, Robert, 207
Reed, Tracy, 233
Reeves, George, 192
Reilly, Charles Nelson, 226
Reiner, Carl, 245
Rennie, Michael, 187
Repp, Stafford, 192
Rettig, Tommy, 241
Reynolds, Burt, 194, 201
Reynolds, Marjorie, 219
Rhodes, Barbara, 149
Richard, Peter Mark, 53
Richards, Beah, 224
Richards, Paul, 175
Rickles, Don, 225
Rigg, Diana, 24, 141, 183
Riley, Jeannine, 150, 230
Rist, Robbie, 212
Ritter, John, 248
Roberts, Pernell, 201
Roberts, Tanya, 202
Roberts, Tony, 181
Robertson, Cliff, 192
Robertson, Dale, 64, 198
Rock, Blossom, 223
Rockwell, Robert, 192, 220
Rodman, Vic, 178
Rodriquez, Abraham, 147
Rogers, Wayne, 202
Romero, Cesar, 186, 192
Romero, Ned, 179
Rooney, Tim, 228
Ross, Anthony, 54
Ross, Joe E., 170
Rossi, Al, 204
Roundtree, Richard, 204
Ruick, Melville, 175
Rush, Barbara, 216
Ruskin, Shimen, 140, 234
Russell, John, 199
Russell, William, 41
Ryan, Fran, 227

Ryan, Irene, 231
Ryan, Mitchell, 53, 95, 177
Ryder, Eddie, 176

Sanders, Beverly, 236
Sanders, Lugene, 113
Santori, Reni, 180
Saunders, Lori, 230
Savage, John, 96
Savalas, Telly, 195
Saxon, John, 178
Schallert, William, 190
Schell, Ronnie, 226
Schrieber, Avery, 229
Scott, Devon, 239
Scott, Jacqueline, 214
Sellecca, Connie, 163
Serling, Rod, 207
Shatner, William, 54, 179, 207
Sheridan, Ardell, 150
Sherman, Bobby, 212
Sherwood, Madeleine, 225
Silla, Felix, 223
Silverheels, Jay, 199
Silvers, Phil, 226
Slattery, Richard X., 245
Slezak, Walter, 192
Sloyan, James, 178
Smith, Jaclyn, 202
Smith, John, 65
Smith, Roger, 204
Smothers, Dick, 165, 246
Somack, James, 233
Sommars, Julie, 226
Sorel, Louise, 235
Sorvino, Paul, 53
Sothern, Ann, 113, 229
Soul, David, 180, 196, 212
Spielberg, David, 233
Stack, Robert, 54, 190, 197
Stacy, James, 65
Stahl, Richard, 247
Stanley, Florence, 149
Stanwyck, Barbara, 198
Statton, Albert, 183
Stefan, Virginia, 185
Stephens, James, 213
Stephens, Loraine, 204
Sterling, Robert, 244
Stevens, Connie, 203
Stevens, Craig, 96
Stevens, Inger, 225
Stevens, Julie, 215
Stevens, Stella, 175
Stevens, Warren, 211
Stevenson, McLean, 225
Stewart, James, 179
Stiers, David Ogden, 235
Stiller, Jerry, 238
Stone, Harold J., 219

Stone, Mary, 218
Stone, Milburn, 201
Strimpell, Stephen, 229
Stuart, Barbara, 226, 236
Sullivan, Barry, 41, 65, 186
Sullivan, Susan, 177
Summers, Hope, 223
Sutorius, James, 215
Sutton, Frank, 124
Sweet, Dolph, 182

Taeger, Ralph, 41, 64
Talbot, Nita, 205
Talman, William, 183
Tar, Justin, 210
Taylor, Elizabeth, 168
Taylor, Jud, 176
Taylor, Kent, 74
Taylor, Robert, 198
Taylor, Rod, 65
Tenafly, Harry, 205
Thinnes, Roy, 178, 206, 209, 212
Thomas, Danny, 164, 218
Thomas, Frank, 179
Thomas, Marlo, 231
Thomas, Michael, 209
Thompson, Ernest, 178
Thompson, Marshall, 188
Thor, Jerome, 184
Thorson, Linda, 183
Tighe, Kevin, 211
Tobias, George, 223
Todd, Daniel, 230
Todd, Joseph, 230
Todd, Michael, 230
Tone, Franchot, 175
Tong, Sammee, 217, 228
Tork, Peter, 229
Totter, Audrey, 177
Towne, Aline, 192
Tracy, Lee, 158
Turner, Lana, 246
Tyler, Beverely, 215
Tyrrell, Ann, 217

Umeki, Miyoshi, 224
Urich, Robert, 233

Vaccaro, Brenda, 74
Valentine, Karen, 93
Van Patten, Dick, 239
Vance, Vivian, 221
Vaughan, Robert, 186
Verdugo, Elena, 113, 179
Vivyan, John, 189

Wagner, Lindsay, 188
Wagner, Lou, 193
Wagner, Robert, 185, 205

Wainwright, James, 53
Walker, Clint, 54, 198
Walker, Nancy, 196, 233, 237
Walston, Ray, 229
Walter, Jessica, 193
Ward, Burt, 192
Ward, Larry, 64
Warden, Jack, 53, 196, 210, 232
Warren, Lesley Ann, 187
Washbrook, Johnny, 242
Washington, Kenneth, 227
Waterman, Willard, 219
Waters, Ethel, 113
Watson, Debbie, 231
Wayne, David, 192
Weatherwax, Rudd, 245
Weaver, Dennis, 195, 201, 241, 245
Webb, Jack, 178, 194
Webster, Chuck, 158
Weld, Tuesday, 220
Wells, Dawn, 123
Wells, Mary K., 215
West, Adam, 191
White, Betty, 245
Whitman, Stuart, 198
Whitmore, James, 74, 180, 209
Whitson, Samuel, 182
Widmark, Richard, 195
Wilcox, Larry, 193
Williams, Clarence, 196
Williams, Guy, 200, 208
Williams, Kathy, 192
Williams, Spencer, 217
Williams, Van, 188
Wilson, Grady, 238
Winchell, Walter, 197
Windom, William, 230
Winter, Lynette, 226
Winters, Roland, 184
Wong, Anna May, 158
Wood, Natalie, 209
Wood, Peggy, 220
Woodell, Pat, 230
Woods, Donald, 231, 244
Wroe, Trudy, 215
Wyatt, Jane, 218
Wyler, Richard, 54
Wynter, Dana, 186

Young, Alan, 162, 241, 242
Young, Gig, 244
Young, Robert, 178
Young, Stephen, 180
Young, Tony, 64
Yung, Victor Sen, 201

Zaremba, John, 185, 208
Zimbalist, Efrem, Jr., 49, 194, 199, 204